The title says it all. Bev Ryan, master book co[...] decades of publishing and writing smarts to guide you all the way from coming up with the best idea for your book to holding the finished product in your hands and successfully getting it out into the world. As well as clear, practical steps for you to follow, underscored with inspirational examples from some of the many women she has personally coached, Bev shares her personal publishing stories and philosophies. Grab your journal, take notes, do the recommended exercises, and watch your book develop and grow with every turn of the page of this wise, power-packed book.

**Jane Teresa Anderson, BSc Hons: dream analyst, author of seven books including *The Dream Handbook* (Hachette)**

In a world where it's getting harder and harder to stand out from the crowd, there is no doubt that writing a book is one of the most powerful ways to actually do that. BUT, to really stand out from the crowd you have to write and publish a great book – and that is where Bev Ryan steps in. In *Smart Women Publish*, Bev offers the right mix of aspirational messaging and down and dirty practical advice, both designed to help get your book written and published. If you've been sitting on the fence, thinking about writing that book, read *Smart Women Publish* and you will find the motivation and the information to make it happen.

**Andrew Griffiths: international bestselling author, global speaker and entrepreneurial commentator**

*Smart Women Publish* is an immensely readable book that will have you racing to your laptop to capture the book that *you* have always wanted to write – but have not known how to begin. Bev Ryan has generously shared the genesis of her own publishing story and very skilfully crafted clear steppingstones to demystify the writing and publishing process. And therein lies the succinct and powerful message from this author. *Smart Women Publish* is uplifting, empowering and inspiring.

Bev is one of those rare individuals who has the skill to draw out the confident voice of others, and she writes with poise, empathy and intelligence to encourage women to express that as an author. Bev's writing and publishing expertise is underpinned by her esteemed reputation as a career coach, public speaker, and facilitator. Bev has achieved her success through hard work and a strong vision.

**Lorraine Merritt: executive mentor, performance coach, author of *Talking the Talk***

Recently I was at a business meeting presenting a proposal and I handed over my self-published book as an introduction. The increase in my credibility with that action was palpable in the room. If you are seeking to enhance your business credibility with your own book, then Bev Ryan has written your perfect how-to guide. *Smart Women Publish* draws on Bev's extensive experience with writing and self-publishing, as well as her years of mentoring and guiding other writers through all things necessary to make their book a reality. Bev's knowledge and assistance were certainly instrumental in making my own book happen.

**Denise Gibbons: author of *Women as Leaders* and women's leadership mentor, chartered accountant and financial planning specialist**

I wish to acknowledge the role Bev Ryan personally played in the creation of my life-changing event, the publication of my first book *Slippin' on the Lino*. Her role in me achieving that dream – which went on to then become a second book, *In Stockmen's Footsteps*, published by a major publisher, Allen & Unwin – cannot be overstated. Neither can the role played by other women friends who supported and encouraged me throughout both processes. This has been my strength. I may have a certain skill, but I have not done what I have done on my own.

**Jane Grieve: business owner, writer, author of *Slippin' on the Lino* and *In Stockmen's Footsteps***

Writing can be a scary ride into unchartered territories and the unknown. With Bev's guidance and support, I was able to find my voice and become a published author. That achievement not only gave me a tremendous sense of accomplishment, but it also gave me a platform to become more visible in my professional world. Bev's new book, *Smart Women Publish*, provides support and practical steps, from planning your book to structuring, designing and marketing it. With this book, you are not alone on this journey of discovery.

**Dolores Cummins: author of *Altitude – two women on Mt Kilimanjaro*, executive leadership specialist**

Putting your story or your expertise into a published book is one of the most personally empowering things you can do. In this book, Bev has carefully crafted a way forward for you, and has answered many of your questions about getting started and getting it done. This book is essential reading for any woman who dreams of writing their own book in order to grow their business. I say just get it, read it carefully, and get started while it is fresh in your mind.

Bev is an extremely experienced professional who offers a complete suite of writing and publishing services. She saved me when I needed editing done quickly, and she did an exceptional job.

**Amanda Bigelow: author of *Powered by Health*, certified health coach and authority on food as medicine**

Do you have a half-written manuscript that you haven't had the courage to complete? Or a book idea that is begging for attention? Bev Ryan, book coach and publisher, provides you with practical hands-on tools in *Smart Women Publish,* and gives you the confidence to begin AND complete your book project. Not only that, she has given you the methodology to complete and publish your book, which in turn gives you another platform on which to promote yourself as an expert in your field. I highly recommend this book if you want to connect, grow and succeed in business.

**Janelle Bostock: CEO of Women's Network Australia**

# SMART
# WOMEN
*Publish*

## Write the book that
## expands your world

# BEV RYAN

Foreword by Dr Lois Frankel, international speaker,
author of *Nice Girls Don't Get the Corner Office*

First published in 2019
Revised in 2021
Brisbane, Australia
www.smartwomenpublish.com

Author: Bev Ryan
Title: *Smart Women Publish – Write the book that expands your world*
ISBN: 9780987078421

Subjects: Business – Self-publishing – Career
Published by smartwomenpublish.com

A catalogue record for this book is available from the National Library of Australia

Disclaimer

The material in this publication is of the nature of general comment only, and does not represent professional advice. It is not intended to provide specific guidance for particular circumstances, and it should not be relied on as the basis of any decision to take action or not take action on any matter which it covers. Readers should obtain professional advice where appropriate, before making any such decision. To the maximum extent permitted by law, the author and publisher disclaim all responsibility and liability to any person, arising directly or indirectly from any person taking or not taking action based on the information in this publication.

This book is dedicated to all women who are
risk takers
light shiners
change makers.

Recognise your worth.
Expand your value.
Release your remarkable.

# CONTENTS

**Part D - Time to Publish and Market**

**Author Spotlights**

**Extras**

# ABOUT THE AUTHOR

Bev Ryan is a trusted non-fiction book coach and book production manager, guiding business and professional leaders to contribute to positive change, demonstrate their expertise, build their credibility, and capture and monetise their IP by writing and publishing quality books.

As the founder and publisher of two nationally distributed magazines, one of which won national and local business awards, Bev had many years' experience coordinating content, editing, design, production, sponsors, sales and distribution.

In 2009, Bev responded to the increasing demand for book guidance and self-publishing services as the trend of business owner as author grew. She has since worked with hundreds of women (and men) in business and professional services by providing publishing workshops, author programs, book coaching and publishing project management services, which include editing, design, print, and online distribution.

Her other experiences as an English teacher (BA, Dip Ed.), career coach, government project officer, kitchen designer and manufacturer, community program manager, world traveller, and parent of four, all add depth and understanding to the work she does with clients from an array of industries and backgrounds.

Bev and her partner live in Brisbane, Australia, adore their blended extended family, and are quite partial to good music, good people, good food, an uncomplicated life – and Nordic noir.

Contact Bev at smartwomenpublish.com

# ACKNOWLEDGEMENTS

Thank you, Geoff, and our unique collective of kind and gifted family – you are my centre.

I am grateful for the contributions to this book from Dr Lois Frankel, the authors in the spotlight segments, and the generous reviewers. I appreciate your trust in my work.

I appreciate and salute the creative people who assist me so well – editors, graphic designers, printers – to ensure we produce quality books. It takes a team.

Thank you too, to the many fascinating and inspired people who have invited me into your creative lives as you have planned, written and published your important books. It truly is a privilege to be part of something so meaningful.

I am so grateful also for encouragement, inspiration and good cheer from the many enterprising, positive people I have surrounded myself with through various supportive business communities and engaging workplaces. You help keep the fire burning.

# HOW TO USE THIS BOOK

Dear Reader

This is more than a book about how to self-publish. It's a book about trusting your value, having the self-belief and discipline to dig deep and create something wonderful, and taking a quantum leap as you push it out into the world.

It is about transforming potential into prosperity.

I suggest you make a decision – the starting point for any new adventure – and begin your publishing journey with this book as your guide.

As well as useful content about planning, producing and leveraging your book, I have added these extra features to assist you to actually get your own book underway as you read:

**Author Spotlights:** Between each chapter you will find a profile of a successful woman who has chosen to self-publish non-fiction in order to grow her business or career. I have intentionally included women you will relate to easily – wonderful women I know personally – so you will be inspired and energised as you read, and will see that you can do this too.

**Journal Exercises:** In Chapter 1 I write about my own life-changing experience after reading a particular book. I know for certain the change only occurred because I purchased a journal to record and expand my awareness as I read that book, and I took time out regularly over a week or two to work through all of the book's exercises thoughtfully. I was fully engaged, and I took action – then went on to become a magazine publisher because of that journal exploration time.

Now I want my book to do the same for you. I have added exercises and plenty of blank pages, so PLEASE purchase a beautiful pen, take time out regularly, respond to the questions I pose at the end of the chapters, explore yourself and your potential, and begin building your own book notes. This serves various purposes:

- You are writing.
- You will become excited about the idea of your own book.
- You are gathering ideas, inspiration and fodder for your book.
- You are engaging your brain in a much more powerful way than just thinking about the questions will ever do.
- You are actually working on your book as you write.

Most importantly though, enjoy the process!
Bev Ryan

---

# FOREWORD

## DR LOIS FRANKEL

When Bev Ryan asked me to write the foreword for her new book, I enthusiastically agreed – even before she shared the topic with me! That's because in the years that I've interacted with her, both in Australia and from the United States, I've come to trust her wisdom, professionalism, practical bent, and sincere desire to be of service to women. Then when she told me this was a book about encouraging women to write and publish, I was even more enthused. I believe self-publishing can change your life. I know, because it changed mine.

For nearly two decades before self-publishing my first business book, I worked as an executive coach with both men and women from *Fortune* 500 corporations around the globe. Flying back to Los Angeles from a coaching session with a client in Washington, DC, I realized that there are many more women who *can't* afford a business coach than ones who *can*. I thought about all of the coaching suggestions I had given to my clients over the years and decided I wanted to share them in a way that would allow any woman to coach herself to success. It was that *pivotal* moment that Bev talks about in this book. On that same plane ride I outlined what would eventually become the bestselling business bible for women.

Over the course of the next six months I wrote the manuscript for what I called *Quit Bein' a Girl*. Most nights after work, weekends, and whenever I found myself with a spare moment during the day, were spent writing. The words and ideas flowed from a depth of knowledge garnered over the course of my life and career. Given that the book was written using a non-traditional format for self-help books, I figured I had no choice but to self-publish. The book did moderately well as I used it as a calling card with clients and potential clients. Then I sent it to a literary agent who loved the idea and sold the rights to the book to a large publisher who promptly changed the name to *Nice Girls Don't Get the Corner Office*. And my life has not been the same since.

Self-publishing helped me gain access to a platform that has been critical to achieving my professional, personal, and financial goals. Having an existing hard copy in the format that I envisioned and believed would suit the lives of busy professional women made it an easier sell to a publishing house. The editors didn't have to picture it; they could hold it in their hands and read it. I knew of other authors who had been the same route – self-publish, then sell. The most obvious benefit of working with a publishing house is having the marketing and publicity departments behind you doing what most authors (including myself) hate doing – selling the book!

Even if *Nice Girls Don't Get the Corner Office* (and its sequel *Nice Girls Don't Get Rich*) hadn't been commercially successful, the books still would have given voice to messages that I felt women needed to hear. Most importantly, I knew these messages had the potential to change women's lives. Before self-publishing, I was touching perhaps a few hundred lives a year. Today, between media interviews, keynote speeches, and training programs, I have the privilege and satisfaction of knowing that I touch thousands.

I share this story with you because I want you to understand that I was no different than you when I started the journey of writing through self-publishing. Every woman has a different reason for writing a book and, in my experience, few women actually follow through on bringing their ideas to fruition. More women than I can count have asked me for advice on how to write a book and get it published. Very few of these women have actually done it. When asked the secret to actually completing a book, my response is always the same: *you must have a message that you want to get out so badly that you cannot live with yourself if you don't say it.* It's almost like a compulsion – something that you cannot not do!

Which brings me back to *Smart Women Publish.* Just as my books coach women to achieve their career goals, this book will coach you to achieve your goals as an author. It doesn't matter if you want to write a book to stimulate business, establish yourself as a subject matter expert, have a product for online or back-of-the-room sales, or because, like me, you simply want to make a difference. Your book complements your professional brand – and we are *all* brands. And remember, your first book may not be your last book, so don't feel the necessity to throw in everything and the kitchen sink.

Bev Ryan, having been there and done it, is the perfect person to take you through each of the steps needed to write and publish your own book. From the seminal idea to forging a message, dealing with your self-doubt, identifying your audience and getting the book out, Bev provides a gentle guiding hand for successfully manoeuvring what can be an overwhelming morass. She's the coach every writer wishes she could have in her life – and now they can.

Don't procrastinate. In the words of Johann Goethe, 'Concerning all acts of initiative and creation there is one elemental truth ... the moment one commits oneself, then providence moves too'.

Lois P. Frankel, PhD
Author of *Nice Girls Don't Get the Corner Office*
Co-founder of the Bloom Again Foundation
www.drloisfrankel.com

*It might have been
done before, but
it hasn't been
done by you!*

~ Elizabeth Gilbert,
in *Big Magic: Creative
Living Beyond Fear*

# INTRODUCTION

Let's expose a few false beliefs about writing and publishing to begin.

- Words always come easily to successful writers.
- They feel no fear.
- Books have to be long to be useful.
- 'Bestseller' status is the only measure of success.
- Writing a book is just a logical process.
- Self-publishing means inferior quality.

To the contrary:

- Even successful (whatever that means) authors like Elizabeth Gilbert (*Eat Pray Love* and *Big Magic*) have times of silence when nothing flows. Nothing. Books happen when an idea germinates; a decision is made; habits are formed; and fear comes along for the ride – in the back seat, or preferably the trunk.
- Some of the most impactful books in recent history have been small (*Don't Sweat the Small Stuff*) or short (*Who Moved My Cheese?*).

- Your business or industry book does not have to be a bestseller to create the ongoing impact you desire. The case studies throughout this book will confirm that for you.
- All books are a beautiful combination of logical thought, determination and creativity. They are an intellectual pursuit and creative design project beautifully wrapped up into one – with a tangible outcome that you can joyfully spread about the world with pride.
- You have access to seasoned industry professionals who will ensure your self-published book has a quality finish equal to others like them sitting proudly on the shelf in any quality bookshop – or in any home or office.

This book is for enterprising women like you, in business or a career, who are excited by the idea of self-publishing a strategic book which fits in with your existing enterprise, or which opens up a new path by quickly raising your profile and expanding your influence.

You are very interested in adding 'author' to your credentials; however, you are more passionate about what a book can do for you AND your readers in the context of your business or profession.

Your book has the potential to become a pivotal tool in expanding your connections, your client base, your income and your opportunities. You should then be mindful of making your book as marketable as possible throughout the entire writing and production process.

These questions that you need to answer from the outset are covered in the pages of this book:

- **What are your holistic goals for the book?** Do you want the book to help grow your personal brand, reputation, career, or business in a specific field?

- **What is the *specific* target market for your book?** The key word here is *specific*. Your answer to this question shouldn't be 'potentially everybody'. Your target market can be segmented by relevant characteristics such as values, aspirations, income, purchasing habits, family situation, geography, interests, talents, education level, occupation, gender, and much more.

- **Why will people want to read your book?** To answer this question, think of content angles or hooks that will generate reader interest and provide solutions to problems. Will it be about a topical subject or in a niche area that is currently not well-serviced by existing books?

- **When will your book be available for purchase and distribution?** Set a realistic goal date and plan out your project step by step to ensure you meet that date.

- **What will your book title and sub-title be?** Decide on a working title early on because you can use this to generate interest.

- **What will the cover look like?** Your book's front cover design and text are vitally important and can be put to good use as you write.

- **What is the sales pitch for your book?** Create a sales blurb suited to your back cover because that will help you determine your content as well, and it too is useful during the writing phase.

- **What content will you include in this book?** Plan this out carefully so that it is a logical progression of ideas, taking your reader from problem or need to a useful solution and call to action.

- **How can you finance the book?** There may be viable ways to raise money to assist with the costs associated with publishing your book, if you feel your budget is tight and will impact the final quality.

- **How will you be able to leverage your book as you write it, and when it is published?** For example, what contacts or networks do you have (or could you develop during the writing and production process) that will help spread the word about your book?

- **What other products or services can you offer because of your book?** How can you bundle your book with higher value products, events, services or programs?

In these pages I will show you why and how to publish a book that will dramatically impact you and your business or career. Choose now to think of that as your first book and be alert to expanding ideas and horizons as you write and create.

In the self-publishing process you will become not just an author, but also a publisher, and open the doors to other book adventures beyond your first publication. Your books can become integral parts of an existing business, or independent profit generators.

PART A

# WHAT A BOOK CAN DO FOR YOU

*There is someone remarkable inside you, someone with a major role still to play in the drama of your life, trying to tell you she hasn't been on the scene yet. She's got the dreams that reflect the unused creativity, untapped brilliance, thwarted adventurousness of your one-of-a-kind brain.*

~ Barbara Sher,
author of *Live the Life you Love*

CHAPTER 1

# IT'S YOUR TIME

I n life, most of us have at least one pivotal moment, a moment that is so crystal-clear in its unequivocal truth that time screams to a stop. My pivotal moment was just that.

It was March 20, 1997, mid-week. I walked through the book section of a suburban department store, focussed on my search for a good cup of coffee.

I needed one. Prior to this, I'd spent a rather distraught hour with a counsellor in a nearby practice, and my emotions threatened to brim over. To be honest, my angst was four-fold, a paralysis-inducing mix of:

- Career-pause
- At-home busy mumming of four
- Fumbling about, trying to find *me* in there again, and
- A yearning for something unidentifiable.

Coffee aromas pulling me on, my eyes lightly scanned gorgeous book covers on the shelves as I walked. I loved them, mainly for their beauty and especially for their comfort factor. Then, suddenly, my pivotal moment materialised. There it was: the book written just for me.

Akin to a neon sign, it stopped me in my tracks with its bright yellow background, flashing words that I swear had been wrenched from my brain and plastered on its cover: *I could do anything if only I knew what it was.* Yes. I had to have it. There was no question.

Soon ensconced with coffee and my shiny yellow beacon, I felt myself lighten as I read Barbara Sher's words. I was normal. I was not alone.

With Sher's book as guidance and my writing journal never far away, over the next few weeks I felt my tension ease and my purpose sharpen: *publish a magazine to help others just like me.*

Then, I worked. Hard.

On 1 January 1998, my very own creation, a nationally distributed print magazine about home-based business, which I named *Work from Home* – no embellishment in that title – sat alongside the big names on magazine shelves in newsagencies across the country.

---

Starting budget – *pretty much zero*; profit from first issue – *affirmative.*

I had found my place at last.

So began my fabulous career transformation, and today, as a mix of publishing manager and coach, I delight in supporting others to find their spark, fuel their fire, face their fears and doubts, and step up to release their remarkable selves through publishing.

Books do change lives. Ms Sher's changed mine. Yours will too.

## WHERE ARE YOU NOW?

In my day-to-day life, I have the privilege of working with many small business owners and professional service providers who see the benefit of self-publishing a book to raise their profile, attract business opportunities, and increase their business revenue.

In my work, I also encounter the opposite.

I recently spoke to a group about career advancement at a professional development day for the environmental engineering industry and asked the audience of highly qualified individuals: 'Have any of you ever considered writing a non-fiction book as a way of standing out in your industry?'

Silence.

None of these individuals (all knowledgeable, highly experienced and extremely talented) had seriously considered it as a career strategy.

But why *not* consider it?

Imagine: You, an expert in your field, armed with a finely honed purpose, a carefully-selected audience and a little bit of resolve, could single-handedly propel your career. Whether you're an employee or business owner, publishing your own non-fiction book could be what your career has been missing for years.

You may even decide during the book planning process that it is time to change careers, establish your own consultancy, or change your business model completely. You can quietly write the book that will launch your new direction while you stay in the safety of your current role.

Here's what publishing your own non-fiction book can do for you:

1.  The process of researching and writing your book, whether it is in your current field or a new direction, will add a stimulating project to your life, sharpen your intellect, awaken you to things you weren't even aware that you didn't know, and by default cause you to become an expert in your area. It may even be more effective than plugging away at a general degree because you think you should.

2.  Writing and researching a book gives you a perfect reason to connect with other experts across the globe, whose work

you admire, and who you might like to quote or include in your book. Doors truly do open that way.

3. Publishing a book will extend you through various steps, from the excitement of the idea to the interesting research, to the hard (but manageable) slog of synthesising knowledge through writing, to the creativity of design and layout. To hold the well-constructed and professionally designed end product in your hands is one of the most rewarding experiences you will ever have – and a great source of pride and kudos.

4. Your book can be the start of a greater body of work that provides a gateway to greater numbers of people, by integrating your intellectual property into such things as various book series, online learning materials, live events, in-depth coaching, implementation, advanced training, teacher certification and more.

## RESISTANCE

A couple of years ago, I enjoyed a night out at a folk music event in a lovely local restaurant in the western suburbs of Brisbane. A charming duo, Chloe and Silas, provided the highlight of the evening.

Their song *Tightrope*, Chloe explained, is about those moments when we want to step out on the wire and go for a new big, scary, precious dream that has us on fire, yet fear still grabs at the back of our shirt to hold us safe. This is Chloe's take on it – much more eloquent than mine:

*One foot on the platform, one foot on the wire;*
*One hand smothers the spark, the other hand fans the fire.*

For me, publishing was the fire. Still is. It can be yours, too.

Resistance, however, is that hand holding your shirt, that voice in your head saying, 'Whoaaa; wait a minute! It's getting scary … I can't do this. Who do I think I am? Why would anybody want to read my book?'

You may already be thinking, 'Me? Write a book? I barely scraped through English in year ten,' or 'Write a book with chapters? I'd get stuck after the second sentence.' And this: 'I'm sure it'll cost way too much money.'

And the big one: 'It's too scary to even think about.'

Fear is a powerful thing, isn't it?

The thought of writing a book is sure to flare up some irrational thoughts. Right now you may be afraid you have nothing useful to say. You are probably afraid that you will be criticised or mocked by your industry peers. You fear that anyone … or everyone … could do a better job of a book than you.

Someone may have told you to keep your intellectual property securely locked up in your own mind, so you fear exposure. You fear that you don't have a qualification that says you can do this – so you are wondering whether you should enrol in yet another course.

You fear that your dream is trivial, and your work has no consequence. After all, anyone can do what you do, right?

Perhaps you think you're too old to start something new? Really? That's the best time to dive into a new and exciting project that makes you feel alive!

You get the drift. (We are silly humans, aren't we? We happily cheer others on while we hold on to the back our own shirt out of fear.)

Barbara Sher, the writer of the book that 'saved' me all those years ago, writes that resistance (or fear) is really just telling us that we need more in order to feel safe when embarking on something new. We need:

- more information so we feel adequately knowledgeable
- better use of existing time instead of saying we never have enough. (Guess what, there is no more to have.)
- a better understanding of resources so we know we have what is required
- alternative thinking so we find ways to fund what we want instead of using the money excuse
- more support to cheer us on and remind us our dreams are important, even when we doubt ourselves.

When we understand that, we are free to find what we need and take small steps forward. That was exactly what I did twenty years ago, when I decided to become a magazine founder with no prior self-publishing experience.

I set a goal with a deadline, asked for the information I needed, found resources and people with the expertise I lacked, created a support group of like-minded people all going after special dreams, then took small steps every day. It's a powerful mix.

## YOU CAN DO THIS

If you're worried about your writing skills or your patently horrible grammar, don't be. There are editors out there who love wrangling language and ideas into shape. And book designers wield those words and imagery into beautiful things on screen, which printers turn into magical entities called books.

Really – why wouldn't you?

Remember too, you're the expert. You know your stuff. That's why people will want to (and currently do) listen to you. Writing and self-publishing your own non-fiction book in your field of expertise is your wheelhouse. It's your cup of tea. (Yes, your publishing guide will also help you avoid clichés.)

Imagine that you're a marine biologist and someone asks you to describe the differences between dolphins and porpoises. Can you write a brief overview in a paragraph in 10 minutes?

Of course you can. Again, you're the expert. As a marine biologist, you'd be a *master* at writing a book on dolphins and porpoises. If you're a university professor, you'll be a rock-solid choice to write a book on how to teach first-year university students. If you're a potter, write *the* book for pottery beginners, just as Patt Gregory, woodwork teacher in Mullumbimby NSW, wrote *Woodwork for Women* to grow her niched business. It worked.

Publishing a book will do wonders for your sense of purpose and value, give you an effective strategy for personal growth, and provide a springboard to consulting, mentoring, public speaking, invitations to join boards, committees and more.

The great news is that you don't need to know *everything* when you start writing your book. You might liken the writing of your book to a low-cost, self-paced study program that may well do more for you than a general university degree could ever do. (Disclaimer: of course there are many professions where only a university degree will do.)

## WHERE ARE YOU IN YOUR CAREER?

If you're a beginner in your career or business, my hat's off to you for considering writing a book. You will learn so much in the process; it will be a sure-fire way to be noticed in the crowd; and will lead to exciting options that may not otherwise come your way.

If you're mid-career, writing a book can give you a jolt of newfound excitement and inspiration, as well as a boost to the speaking lectern. Imagine interviewing and including the insights of respected people in your field who you have always admired. (And they will now know who you are – especially when you mail them a copy of your book, with their name in it.) Imagine pouring your knowledge out onto the pages of something you're exceedingly passionate about. (Trust me, few things could ever be this exciting.)

If you are still blooming while others your age may be slowing, you are my kind of person! I constantly meet women who are excited to be launching a new business at a time when some their age are retiring. They have realised it's time to do their thing, and that their best days are right now. (After all, it really takes that long to finally figure it all out!) In fact, Australian women aged over 65 are starting their own businesses at a rate unmatched by any other generation in the last 10 years, according to research from Bankwest in 2013. The NBN™ Silver Economy Report in 2017 confirmed this trend.

If you have a lifetime's treasure of knowledge and experience, writing and self-publishing your own non-fiction book in your area of expertise may be just the thing you need, whether you are:

- in the early days of a new business
- looking for a way to leave a legacy and a footprint before or during retirement
- seeking a way to stay active in your industry, on boards and committees
- looking for a meaningful project in retirement
- looking for a transformative experience (because, believe me, writing a book is just that).

Publishing preserves your hard-earned wealth of knowledge and experience for the benefit of those coming after you. You leave a footprint and a legacy. Publishing also removes the frustration of invisibility – the feeling that in the world's eyes, your best days are over after a certain age.

It's an adventurous, fun, creative process, with amazing repercussions, this self-publishing gig, and it stretches you in wonderful ways.

## WHAT DRIVES YOU?

Every now and then I am reminded of the incredible swings of emotion I experienced when, back in 1997, I first set myself a goal to self-publish (with no prior industry experience) a national magazine for people just like me – would-be home-based business owners. (In 1997, not a lot of people were working from home, but boy, didn't a lot of us want to!)

I teetered from sheer excitement and anticipation to abject terror. *Who the hell am I to think anyone would want to read what I want to produce? What qualifications do I have? Do I even have time for this? Or the necessary talent?*

Never had I pushed myself to that point before. I'd always kept my feet fairly planted on trusted soil. Going public through publishing was a very big deal in so many ways – and learning to deal with those extremes of fear and fancy was the best thing I have ever done.

Take the time to identify the emotional core of your goals and dreams – essentially, the true heart of your desire. Identifying what you love best about the idea of writing a book will help fuel your fire.

Take time to dream and build an image of you, the author. What is sitting at your core?

Do you need this for yourself? Does someone else need your book?

Odds are, the answers are 'Yes, and yes'.

---

*Now, let's get to work. Your first exercise is on the next page, so use the pages provided here to begin recording and expanding your own awareness. Or you may prefer to purchase a beautiful 'book journal' of your own in which to collect your book ideas.*

# JOURNAL EXERCISE

## DESIRE

*Your desire is revealing. Have a straightforward conversation with it. It's likely to tell you that you want X because it will make you feel complete. Or that you want Y because it will make you feel powerful. Or that you want Z because it will make you feel free.*

~ Danielle LaPorte

*What is your desire telling you?*

Read the words above from Danielle LaPorte, author and coach. Write your thoughts here, really tapping into the pull inside you that has brought you to this book about publishing. Reveal your true desire for your future here.

# MARYANNE LEIGHTON

*MaryAnne is a freelance writer and educator on large animal rescue, living in South East Queensland. She writes here about her second book,* Equine Emergency Rescue - a guide to Large Animal Rescue.

I was determined to retain control over all aspects of publishing and marketing this book and lost a lot of sleep agonising over how I would find funds to publish independently. As I agonised, I learnt I was to receive a small inheritance, and this paid for book design and printing the first 1000 copies. Twelve months later, sales of the first edition paid for the second edition of 2000 copies, and in February 2015, I was able to print the third edition of a further 2000 copies. I totally control the sale of my book (including giveaways and discounts), updates and new editions, and I have also developed my own training package based on the content of my book.

I went from being an introverted writer who preferred being in the background and absolutely refused to speak publicly, to an astonished but assured public speaker and workshop presenter. I discovered I can talk with passion about the things that engage me most. I was even a speaker at the 5th International Large Animal Rescue conference in 2013. Who, me? Yes, me!

I partnered with the not-for-profit Queensland Horse Council Inc., the then peak body for the horse industry in Queensland. This partnership exposed my book and my work to the 90,000 people on QHC's mailing list and gave me the protection of their Public Liability and Personal Indemnity Insurances as I delivered one-day Large Animal Rescue workshops throughout Australia and New Zealand under the QHC banner. Sadly, QHC is now in abeyance, and I am on my own with my own insurance cover, but I am deeply grateful for the years they worked with and supported me.

*Equine Emergency Rescue – a guide to Large Animal Rescue* has a huge impact on readers as they discover how easily they can be injured or killed while attempting to rescue a trapped large animal. It is a revelation when I use Emergency Management terms to describe a trapped horse as a 'hazardous material, a dangerous object that may explode without warning'. I show rescuers how to keep themselves safe and avoid injuring or killing the trapped casualty by using simple techniques that use the large surface area and skeletal strength of the animal's torso. These techniques avoid tissue damage and trauma to the horse's delicate structures and increase the chance of a successful rescue.

As a direct result of writing and self-publishing this book, since 2012 I have conducted one-day Large Animal Rescue workshops throughout Australia and New Zealand for emergency responders, police, veterinarians, RSPCA and stock inspectors, animal control officers, horse owners and others. Every person who attends a workshop receives a copy of my book as course material.

I give powerful, compelling presentations on Large Animal Rescue to organisations and groups, and at AGMs, and sell books after the presentation. I locally manufacture, import and sell Large Animal Rescue equipment. I am the Asia Pacific distributor of Resquip Rescue products manufactured in the UK. In 2014 I introduced an Aussie inventor to Resquip, and we are selling his product worldwide. I am also working with Resquip to develop more products for the international Large Animal Rescue market.

In the eight years since I independently published *Equine Emergency Rescue*, I have sold close to 5000 copies. It has been a wonderful and exciting eight years and there is not a thing I would have changed.

www.equineER.com

*It's important that you get clear on the benefits you want to achieve from your book before you begin the process. When the writing gets tough, you need to be able to imagine yourself getting the things you want out of life as a result of your published book.*

~ Daniel Priestly,
in *Become a Key Person of Influence*

## CHAPTER 2

# THE POWER OF PUBLISHING

W hat is it about wanting to publish a book that unearths a deep longing in so many individuals?

Ever since Johannes Gutenberg constructed his printing press in 1440 with his own hands, people (like you!) have been gripped by the notion of adding new dimensions of financial reward, excitement, achievement, connection, growth and contribution to their lives.

When you publish a book, you can be as brilliantly creative as you wish and can stretch yourself to your limits and beyond – and yet, at the same time, for those who crave direction and order, it is a logical process.

Your book can roam the world and maybe take you along for the ride. A book I edited in 2018, *Cattlemen in Pearls*, was gifted personally to Anne, HRH The Princess Royal, during an international agricultural event in Canada, and has found its way to Buckingham Palace – and I have a copy of the official thank-you letter to prove it.

Your book can introduce you to people you would never have met otherwise. Give generously and be open to ideas for collaborations and win-wins.

In terms of your business, your book is actually a low-cost item for purchasers who may have never heard of you, or who may want more of what you offer. There is little risk attached for the buyer as it's an easy and familiar purchase, and a book by its very nature says trust and value. And it has longevity and transferability.

It would be difficult to think of another product you could create or develop that offers these benefits to your clients:

- low purchase cost
- high perceived value
- high trust factor
- easy entry to you and your business
- low risk investment

Your book provides a buy-and-try entry option to interested people who will show low resistance to such a purchase. Most people love books – particularly those that show empathy and relevance to the reader. Show that you understand the reader's situation, and offer something of value to them, meeting them where they are.

Some will later invest again with you in other parts of your business because they feel they now know you and trust you. A good book will do that. And some of those people may eventually move into your business inner circle, which requires the highest level of trust, developed over time.

You build ongoing loyalty by providing transformation through your book and your other products and services. You enhance your customer's life and expand their possibilities, enabling them to take what they have learned from you and go on to impact their own world.

Here are some more good reasons to take this publishing thing seriously:

- Writing your book requires you to get total clarity about who you are, what you do, who you want to work with, and what you care about. It can take you back to square one – and even pivot a business completely.
- You will feel you are adding lasting value to the world through your work.
- Gather your existing content and modify for use in your book, or work the other way. Your book can be the launching point for other products and services, such as live workshops, podcasts, events, programs or courses, or

recorded versions sold digitally.

- Apply to speak at larger events than you have ever done before. You may be invited to speak at events and conferences locally and much further afield when your messages are relevant and linked to bigger issues. (Bronwyn Reid, featured in an Author Spotlight before Chapter 13, has spoken in Singapore about her topic of expertise – environmental sustainability – at Asia's leading annual mass participation sports conference. Helen Baker, in the Author Spotlight before Chapter 15, presented at a law conference in Paris.)

- Reach out to key people and influencers in your field during preparation and writing, ask for input or commentary, and be generally welcomed. (Thank you, Dr Frankel, for writing a Foreword for this book.)

- Begin promoting your book before it even comes out, to raise visibility, authority and anticipation, as well as pre-launch sales.

- Use your book to develop your brand and help potential clients understand what you're about, and how you can be valuable to them.

- Benefit from the power of partnerships by giving or selling copies of your book to businesses you partner with, for them to use in their promotions, events and marketing.

- As a published author, people will begin to see you as a leader in your field, which opens opportunities to review your pricing and the type of work you prefer to do.

- Publishing and leveraging your book successfully will require you to stretch and challenge yourself personally and professionally, and will ultimately elevate your self-image.

# INDEPENDENT PUBLISHING

There has been massive growth in self-publishing over the last fifteen years. Advances in technology and the growth and ease of independent endeavours across all creative areas, including music, film and art, have given control and freedom back to the creator.

Reassuringly, and contrary to early predictions when e-books became popular, the print book is not dying. According to sales tracking service Nielsen BookScan, 55.5 million physical books worth A$1.07 billion were sold in Australia in 2017, up from 54.6 million books worth A$1.06 billion in 2016. (This figure includes bookstore sales, academic book sales and online retail sales, including The Book Depository – but cannot track individual sales by independent authors.)

Booktopia, Australia's online book seller and print distributor, reported a 28% increase in new book sales during the 2020 financial year, with total sales topping $165 million for the first time. Booktopia founder and CEO, Tony Nash stated in 2020 that the growth of online purchasing of physical books has been increasing steadily, year on year for many years.

The genre of adult non-fiction showed the largest growth in America in 2018, with paperback, audiobooks and hardbacks the preferred formats, according to the Association of American Publishers. They also report that over 1.8 billion print books were sold by US publishers in 2018, and nearly one-in-five Americans now listen to audiobooks.

# DO IT WELL

Like anything you do in a professional capacity that will build and enhance your brand, though, you have to do it well.

Do not:

- include everything you know
- present badly written material by saving on editing costs
- use an ugly book cover that screams DIY: even simple design ideas require skill, and lack of it definitely shows.
- risk cheap production that falls apart
- write without any thought to what your readers want
- assume 'everyone' should/will read your book
- use inflated language that becomes meaningless
- ask advice from the wrong people
- rely solely on book sales as your only pay-off
- assume the media will be excited just by your book.

# THE REALITY OF COMMERCIAL PUBLISHING

The major advantages commercial publishers offer are an established distribution network and potentially a marketing budget to help promote a specific book. However, it will be difficult to get your book published by a commercial publisher unless you are in one or more of the following categories:

- You are an established author with proven sales of previous books.
- You are a well-known and acknowledged subject matter expert in your field.
- You are a celebrity, or you (or your book) have the potential to generate significant media exposure and publicity.

There are valid reasons for this approach, as commercial publishing is a risky business. Like self-publishers, they generally bear all of the costs of book production, sales and marketing. The retail book publishing industry generally operates on a 'sale or full return rights' basis. This means that commercial publishers only receive payment for books that retailers actually sell. Retailers are able to return any unsold print stock to the publishers, who generally are forced to pulp that stock, or at best, sell it at heavily discounted prices to book 'remainder' operators.

Retail bookstores are also struggling in the online environment, with store closures common in recent times. It is highly competitive for publishers to get shelf space in retail stores, with retailers themselves demanding high profile authors and/or books to stock. They will also often negotiate rebates and higher price discounts in return for providing premium shelf space (e.g. a window location).

To minimise all of the above risks, commercial publishers therefore like to publish 'sure things' as much as possible: this includes sometimes offering successful self-publishers a contract when they see potential for a mutually profitable arrangement, as mentioned by Dr Frankel in the Foreword to this book.

# SELF-PACED LEARNING

You have spent your lifetime gathering and collecting and mixing and practising and perfecting and heading towards the edge to proclaim your knowledge, and backing off again.

If you wish to build or progress your career or business around an area of interest and expertise that does not have a critical formal qualification as an entry requirement, I suggest you take the bold step of publishing in that field to establish your name and credentials.

You will embark upon one of the best self-paced learning programs available to you, and the end result will be a real-life tangible product which shows the world you know your stuff.

A quality book can propel your credentials and solidify your place in your field, guaranteed.

# AN ALTERNATIVE PATH

As a student at the University of Queensland (during the last century, I might add) I spent many hours – some fruitful, some not – amidst the towering shelves of some very serious-looking academic books. No eye-catching dust covers there, just dark, foreboding, uninviting tomes of knowledge.

I remember wondering at the time whether many of those books would perch there without a human eye ever venturing into their hidden world. It was a sad consideration, really.

Decades later, I was invited to speak at a 'Women, Work, Education' Conference run by the Australian Federation of Graduate Women Inc, at that same university. I found myself in a room of very learned women with esteemed positions across academia, government, community services and industry.

It was an intimidating audience, given that I had taken the path of least resistance across that university's well-maintained quadrangles many years before.

Fortunately, I had realised many years ago that I can only be me when presenting, so I let my story come forth confidently, and took the bold opportunity to espouse my theory – fully aware of the minefield I was stepping into – that indeed, self-publishing a commercially viable book in your field of expertise may well do as much for your career as an academic qualification.

Stern faces, unmoved, stared back at me as I spoke.

'That went down well,' I thought sardonically as I sat down again in the speakers' row at the conclusion.

The event came to a close shortly after, and amidst the milling crowd I saw a beautiful young woman approaching me with a radiant smile and excited eyes. 'I just want to thank you,' she said. 'I am a single mum and I have been yearning to do my master's degree, but I just can't afford it. When you spoke about writing a book instead, I got so excited because that's my answer! I've been furiously making notes about my book ideas and I'm sorry, but I didn't hear the end of your talk.'

'Job done!' I thought.

# A DEGREE IS NO GUARANTEE

A formal qualification does not always guarantee doors will open.

However, a researched and well-produced book on a specific topic, for the right audience, with useful ideas and your name on the front, may be a perfect conversation starter. Immediately it says 'disciplined, innovative, entrepreneurial, knowledgeable, independent thinker, and a motivated doer' who is not waiting for permission from others to pursue their dreams.

Lisa-Marie Kerr, the Brisbane-based author of *Get Job Ready: A teen's guide to getting their first job*, wrote her book in 12 weeks, after realising teenagers needed some sensible guidance to help them get their first job.

After her book was released, Lisa-Marie received good media coverage, including an interview on Sunrise, and was often asked to deliver workshops and speak at events. She was very aware though that she had no formal qualifications in this field, however an unexpected opportunity soon presented itself.

A university lecturer saw her speak about her book at a dinner event and later asked her about her own career aspirations. Because of that conversation and her book, she went on to study a Post Graduate Certificate in Career Development, without an undergraduate qualification. Her book was seen as evidence of her skill, passion and dedication.

The book is now in more than 500 schools and libraries across the country.

---

# JOURNAL EXERCISE

## PURPOSE

*It's never too late. Your writing will only get better as you get older and wiser. If you write something beautiful and important, and the right person somehow discovers it, they will clear room for you on the bookshelves of the world – at any age.*

~ Elizabeth Gilbert

To confirm your choice to write a non-fiction book as your best decision ever, let's do a quick exercise. Chose all of the reasons below that match your purpose. Expand on them in the blank pages that follow (or in your own journal) so you can refer back to them as a reminder if you feel yourself losing purpose as you work on your book. Add any other burning reasons you may be harbouring.

☐ Share my knowledge and make a difference by positively impacting others
☐ Be seen as an expert on my topic and be invited to a larger platform
☐ Differentiate myself, be more visible and grow my business
☐ Find paid board positions where my professional expertise is valued
☐ Stop trading time for money and leverage my assets

- ☐ Attract good clients, partners and teams because I am seen as a leader in my field
- ☐ Kickstart a new career or business as I launch my book
- ☐ Live the life of an author, working from home and travelling to book fairs and conferences
- ☐ Capture my hard-earned career experience and mentor others who are beginning
- ☐ Capture all of my intellectual property into book form, then develop other products from that
- ☐ Write my thoughts and memories down for my family and friends, and leave a legacy
- ☐ Share my message or story that I need to tell the world
- ☐ Publish my existing reams of writing, and put them into book form
- ☐ Write for therapy
- ☐ Do self-paced learning in my field and publish a user-friendly book rather than a thesis
- ☐ Capture others' stories, knowledge and experience
- ☐ Feel personal significance, accomplishment and confidence

# JANE HANCKEL

*Jane is an author, educator and social entrepreneur, living in northern New South Wales. She is the author of* Growing Greener Children – Eco Parenting *and other books.*

Writing the initial draft of *Growing Greener Children – Eco Parenting* started one Friday evening and continued non-stop over the weekend after a trip to Sydney for our project. I had repeatedly seen businesses advertising 'eco' services and realised that Eco Parenting summed up both the ecological and holistic nature of our project – *InspirED, Education for a New Era*. The book took a further eight months to expand, research and refine. We were delivering successful holistic early childhood and parenting programs in socially and economically disadvantaged communities across Australia, and the book was a useful tool to articulate the principles and evidence of the work relating to the importance of diet, lifestyle and environment, and children's wellbeing.

I was aware of the need to have the scientific research within the book overseen by an environmental health scientist. I was referred to Jo Immig, an environmental scientist and coordinator of the National Toxic Network, who also lived in the Bryon Shire in northern NSW. Jo had earlier published a book called *The Toxic Playground* about children's health and the environment.

We self-published *Growing Greener Children* using Sunfly Printing, Guangzhou, China, which did an excellent printing job and were competitively priced.

Looking back, the most difficult aspects of self-publishing were both attempting to do the design work on the book myself, as well as the subsequent promotion and marketing.

*Growing Greener Children* is continuing to play a pivotal role in my career and business life, and I have spoken at national and international conferences about how to improve the quality of childhood.

One of the unexpected benefits of publishing *Growing Greener Children* was the extremely positive response from the academic community. This led to my involvement with Professor Leonie Segal, Health, Economics and Social Policy, University of South Australia. The feedback and support enabled me to research the broader aspects of our programs, confirming the critical necessity for our project's health and wellbeing initiatives. This has led to a much stronger basis for developing the online educational areas of InspirED.

Our company has gone on to publish *Parenting as an Art: The Art of Raising Happy, Healthy, Creative Children* which has been translated and published in Vietnam and China. My third book, *Spontaneous Acts of Love*, a book of meditations and reflections for parents has just been published, initially as an e-book.

www.inspirededucation.com.au

*You cannot out-perform your self-image. Improve your image and you will improve your results.*

~ Karen Brook,
global results mentor

## CHAPTER 3

# SET YOURSELF UP FOR SUCCESS

I t is an oft-quoted statistic in the publishing world that 90 percent of people want to write a book in their lifetime. (I cannot confirm the source or accuracy of that figure, so let's regard it as an estimate.) I am also very interested to know how many of that 90 percent actually publish a book that has a positive impact.

Very few, it seems. So what gets in the way of success?

Whether an already busy person hopes to write a fiction or non-fiction book, there will be common factors determining their outcome:

- Is it a vague hope or fantasy, or is it a true goal?
- Do they make a decision, even though they do not yet know how?
- Do they set a deadline or completion date?
- Are they excited and enlivened by their goal to be a published author?
- Or do they allow self-doubt to dictate their actions?
- Do they do what it takes to find the information, resources and assistance they need?
- Do they set a high standard for their work and ensure quality outcomes?
- Do they think, feel and act like a successful author?

I am sure you can quickly see how many things in the list above have been pivotal to your successes to date – and why other fancies have flown by in the wind.

So let's assume you have decided now that you DO want to publish a quality book within a reasonable time frame, and let's focus on ways you can ultimately get what you want – status as a published author of a book that impacts your preferred audience and brings extra joy into your life.

# WRITE DOWN YOUR GOALS

In her practical and inspiring book *Write It Down, Make It Happen*, Henriette Anne Klauser explains how simply writing down your life goals is the first step towards achieving them. In her book, she includes stories of ordinary people who witnessed large and small miracles unfold after they performed the basic act of clarifying their dreams and putting them on paper.

Jim Carrey, an American actor, wrote himself a cheque for $10 million for services rendered, while he struggled to find acting work as a newcomer. Now an internationally-recognised actor, Carrey makes more than $20 million for each individual film.

Scott Adams, creator of the *Dilbert* comic strip, continually wrote, 'I will become a syndicated columnist'. Obviously, that dream came to fruition; *Dilbert* is syndicated in more than 2,000 newspapers worldwide.

Finally, Suze Orman, a world-renowned author and financial whiz, wrote daily when she began many years ago, 'I am young, powerful and successful, producing at least $10,000 a month'. She lived her words and became a lasting success story.

Research has also validated that successful people journal – or that journaling impacts success. In a study many years ago, conducted with 63 recently-unemployed professionals – 'Expressive Writing and Coping with Job Loss' – those assigned to write about the thoughts and emotions surrounding their job loss (expressive writing) were re-employed more quickly than those who wrote about non-traumatic topics or who did not write at all. The study simply asked the writing participants to write for 20 minutes a day for five days. Eight months after the writing assignment,

- 52.6% of those experimental subjects who were asked to do expressive writing had accepted full-time positions.
- Only 23.8% of writing control subjects (keeping a diary about job search practices) had accepted full-time jobs.
- Only 13.6% of non-writing control subjects had accepted employment.

There have been many studies on this subject, all reporting positive results on participants' lives in various ways, including mental and physical health. So how does this work?

* * *

I invited Karen Brook, the Australian-based top-performing results coach globally with the Proctor Gallagher Institute (based in Canada), also a pilot and a friend, to explain this for you at a deeper level:

*Writing causes thinking, thoughts cause feelings, feelings influence behaviour, and behaviour produces results. As you begin to write, you begin to form pictures in your mind; and as you write in positive terms in the present tense, you begin to form positive pictures on the screen of your mind.*

*These pictures begin to program the cybernetic mechanism of your mind, or the 'servo-mechanism', which is like a goal-seeking device keeping you on course to a particular destination.*

*The easiest way to explain how the cybernetic mechanism of your mind functions, and why it's so important to understand, is to think of the global positioning system (GPS) and autopilot in an aircraft. The pilot programs the GPS with an end destination, and no matter how off-course the aircraft might get, the autopilot brings it back on course thanks to the cybernetic mechanism of the GPS. If the pilot decides to change the final destination they must update the coordinates in the GPS, otherwise the aircraft will ultimately keep tracking towards the old destination.*

*This exact process happens to all of us: our destination is a self-image goal programmed in our subconscious mind. How we really see ourselves is set in our subconscious. That is where we will end up heading, no matter how hard we try to go in another direction – our GPS is set!*

*It is a common misconception that to change results, behaviour must change. While an element of that is true, behaviour is a secondary cause of results. The primary cause of your results is the self-image you have programmed in the deepest part of your mind – your subconscious.*

*A person actually has two self-images: they have the image they project to the outside world – how they walk, how they talk, how they dress and comb their hair – and they have the inner image which is ultimately reflected in their outer image. The inner image is made up of beliefs at a very deep level, and will dictate the kind of opportunities a person attracts, how much they earn, the kind of relationships they will create, their logic and many other things. For a person to change their results, they must consciously and deliberately build a new self-image of the person they wish to become, and begin to program the new image into their subconscious mind through repetition.*

*The same is true for you and your goals. If you do not update the programming in your mind, you will keep getting the same results.*

*Begin today to build a new self-image of yourself as a highly successful, published author making the impact you want to have and earning the amount of money you really want to earn.*

*In your Book journal begin to visualise and write your new self-image, as you want to be 12 months from now. Use the exercise at the end of this chapter to guide you.*

*Once you complete your new author self-image script, written in the present tense using positive language, with a goal date, begin at once to read and write it out at every opportunity you get. Challenge yourself to write it every day for 90 days and notice the positive influence it has on every area of your life!*

(Karen can be found at www.karenbrook.com.au.)

# THE VALUE OF BOOK COACHING

Coaching and mentoring are proven ways to help beginners re-set their self-image and enhance performance in any field. Coaching is tailored for the individual, meets them at their level, and moves them to a defined goal of their choice.

Many people talk about writing a non-fiction book – or travelling to the Northern Lights – but few even start the trip! Of those who do begin a book, a large number give up along the way because they have little or no support, few skills, and a lack of experience.

Others begin to falter as they approach the point where their work has the real possibility of going public in the world. At this point, their self-image lets them down. Their paradigms are telling them loudly that they should know their place.

A book coach works with people privately, sometimes in a one-off kick-start session, or on an ongoing basis, to guide and encourage them through the process. It is a fact that people who choose to work with a book coach say they may never have achieved their success without that support.

There are many ways a good book coach can add value:

- sorting through topic options and helping you decide which book you will write first
- dealing with challenges like writer's block, procrastination and indecision
- helping you understand your market and how to reach them
- demystifying the publishing process and options
- guiding you on style and format, as well as your all-important book cover
- connecting you with the other expertise you require, such as editors, designers, etc.
- showing you how to get the best return for your money and your efforts.

With expert guidance, your chances of writing AND completing your own excellent book increase enormously.

*(Refer to 'Publishing Assistance' in the final pages of this book for a link to book coaching support with this author.)*

———————

*It's journalling time. The next exercise gives you permission to dream big. Let go of any nagging doubts and obstacles. Wave your magic wand and let yourself imagine your world as you would love it to be. Write your responses in that state of mind.*

# JOURNAL EXERCISE

## FUTURE SELF

Here in this journal space, or your own book, write out your responses in glorious detail – so much detail that you feel excitement, satisfaction, confidence and anticipation building.

Imagine it is two years from now. You have launched your book.

*It is <date>* _____

*and I am the author of a book about* _____

_____

Describe exactly who you are now, what your life looks like, and how you feel.

Let your mind wander; create the fantasy. This is the first stage in the creation process.

Start every paragraph with *I am so happy and grateful now that* ...

Think about the many different areas of your life. Here are some areas you might wish to include in your new author self-image script:

- ☐ Your book, the launch, the sales, the feedback and the income you have generated
- ☐ Other areas of your business
- ☐ The people who have been impacted by your book
- ☐ The people you have met and the new friendships you have made
- ☐ Your home, where you are living, how you holiday and where you holiday
- ☐ The amount of money you earn, how grateful you feel for earning this money
- ☐ Your personal appearance, how you dress, walk and talk

Write. It. Down. Repeat. You'll be amazed at the power of this small step.

Your writing, in and of itself, has the power to motivate you, spark you and set you on a successful path. It seems it sets your brain on fire.

Most importantly, watch your book unfold.

AUTHOR SPOTLIGHT

# DR MARIA BOULTON

*Dr Boulton is a GP, company director, AMA Qld Council of General Practice Chair, and public speaker, based in Brisbane, Queensland. She is the author of* Mum's Guide to Pregnancy.

I wrote my book for women who are contemplating a pregnancy or who are pregnant. I have used my experience as a doctor working in Australian general practice over the last 16 years to help women through the pregnancy rollercoaster.

The most difficult aspect of writing my first book was finding the time to do it. Between running a business, caring for patients and spending time with my family, it was sometimes difficult to carve out the time to just sit and write. I am so glad I did though. I didn't know anything about publishing, so I sought Bev Ryan's book coaching services to guide me through the process.

*Mum's Guide to Pregnancy* is an extension of what I do every day as a GP. I am a big advocate of education, so that is a big focus of my clinic, Family Doctors Plus, which I co-founded with Dr Fiona Raciti in 2016. Then in 2017 our new business model won the prestigious Telstra Queensland Business of the Year Award, which was a real honour.

In the business we hold regular education sessions for the local community. I have been a regular guest on The Afternoon Program on ABC Radio Brisbane, discussing the latest in health news affecting the local community. My book allows me to continue with this passion, as well as give women and their partners more detailed information about preparing for pregnancy and the birth process.

Something that I did not expect was the immense sense of accomplishment that, as a busy working mother, I was able to complete and publish my book. Another unexpected joy was the awesome book launch party, where people I care about came to celebrate with me.

www.drmariaboulton.com.au

*... the older I get, the less impressed I become with originality. These days, I'm far more moved by authenticity. Attempts at originality can often feel forced and precious, but authenticity has quiet resonance that never fails to stir me.*

~ Elizabeth Gilbert,
*Big Magic: Creative Living Beyond Fear*

CHAPTER 4

# WHO WANTS WHAT YOU HAVE?

I f you bring a combination of passion, knowledge and experience together, and package that into a book with a moving message for people you understand, you too can make a meaningful impact on the world.

Too often though, writers mistakenly believe that if they write a book about everything they know, everyone will want to read it. Not so.

Write a book that's informative and useful, with the right content for the right people, then yes, those people will want to read your book

... or go to your website for content, or follow you on social media, or contact you directly for assistance, or ask you to speak at the business conference.

Planning the best book to publish first – after all, most of us have more than one book in us – requires you to consider the following combination:

The subject area/topic you would love to spend time with

PLUS

who is most motivated to seek information/answers/help now (i.e. read your book/seek coaching/come to your events, etc.)
PLUS

who can afford what you offer

PLUS

your understanding of their true problems

PLUS

what solutions you can offer in your content.

Think long and hard about what you can offer the world in your book. We all are a glorious mixture of energy and attributes, including the tough lessons we learned the hard way during negative experiences: they make us stronger and wiser, and give us even more to share.

Here's a quick list of what most of us have in our rucksacks:

- knowledge that we have gathered through formal education, and informally
- many years of career experience in various roles and companies, across several industries
- our own individual interests and passions that light us up, some of which can be quite delightfully obscure
- our skills – the things we are innately good at or have learned along the way
- our unique viewpoints, formed over our lifetime, and influenced by our upbringing, schooling, spiritual philosophies, travel, people we have met, and observations of the world
- experiences that we have survived or conquered only by digging deep ... very deep
- connections who offer valuable insight and knowledge, and when included in a book, offer greater value than we do alone
- resources that we may have already produced, or written in conjunction with others, that can be drawn on.

We also offer insights and solutions. While we may not be able to solve every problem, we all have the ability and expertise to suggest or provide inspiration and/or solutions in certain situations for certain people.

If you are unsure what you will write about and who exactly your book will appeal to, let's do a little digging. Pull out your Book journal and beautiful pen and get to work.

1. **What do you care about?**

   - What issues or debates or news items cause you to react or become upset?
   - What articles, books, movies attract your attention?
   - Who do you admire, that you may already know or may have never met? Why?

2. **What has honed you?**

   - What difficult times have you come through that have made you stronger and wiser?
   - Describe the events, as well as your personal strengths and knowledge that got you through them. (Take full credit – you may never have acknowledged your own skills in these situations before.)

3. **What is your ideal life?**

   - In your ideal day or week, who would you love to be working with, and how would you do that?

4. **What problems can you help solve?**

   - Describe the types of people or causes you enjoy helping.
   - What are their greatest underlying problems or desires?
   - How can you assist?

# YOUR IDEAL READER

Visualise someone sitting down to read your book over a coffee, with pen in hand to make notes, as they excitedly find the help and inspiration they have been seeking. Who is this person?

- A busy mum of four seeking help with her career, as I once was when I found Ms Sher's books?
- An advertising executive who's trying to understand the new world of digital marketing?
- A burnt-out manager who is tired of dealing with a high turnover in her young employees?
- A mature woman seeking extra income streams?
- An artist who wants to know how to teach others?

People fall into diverse groups in terms of age, activity, interests, life stage, needs, wants, frustrations, problems, leisure activities – the list goes on and on.

At the end of this chapter you will begin to zoom in on your potential readers so that you get a really clear picture of the people you are writing for. I'm not big on dehumanising labels, but some call this your avatar.

Once you have completed that exercise, begin gathering images of a businesswoman, a mechanic, a stressed working dad, an artist, a rural woman, a teenager – whoever you are writing your book for. You might find a number of pictures of different individuals who you think fit the profile and make a collage. After all, none of us are one-dimensional.

Put these images in this journal, a notebook, a Pinterest page, or a folder in your gather ideas, jot down notes, collect stories and so much more. Build a visual of your ideal readers, with notes about their lifestyle, their desires, their needs and wants, and the problems they want help with.

Imagine sitting with this person and talking to them over coffee, as a friend would. They express some concern about the way things are going for them. What do you ask them? What do they tell you? What do they ask you? What suggestions do you give them?

Ultimately you want your book to feel like a friend to readers – warm, wise and supportive. And sometimes bluntly honest. Seize any opportunity you have to speak with people you feel may be interested in your book and ask them questions so you understand them better.

## CHOOSE A CLEAR NICHE

Let's use a real example to illustrate the importance of selecting a clearly defined audience for your book. Author Julie Jansen first published this successful career book, *I Don't Know What I Want, But I Know It's Not This: A Step-by-Step Guide to Finding Gratifying Work* in 2003 with Penguin Books. They have published revised editions in 2010 and 2016.

The book blurb in Amazon indicates that "In this fully revised and updated edition of *I Don't Know What I Want, But I Know It's Not This*, career coach Julie Jansen shows how anyone—whether you're unhappy with your job, or without one—can implement a real and satisfying transformation".

However several reviews like this one indicate that the book is not really for 'everyone' after all: "This book has some good advice and helped me to think more about what I am looking for in a job, but I often felt alienated as I was reading because the only examples the author presents are people from the corporate world. The examples should have been more diverse. People from all work environments struggle with these questions and it would have been much more helpful to see them profiled here."

I want you to understand three things here:

1. The problem is not with the book content: the problem is that the author obviously does not clearly indicate in the title, sub-title or marketing blurbs that the audience she is writing to are people in corporate or professional careers. Looking at the reviews, those people seem to love it.
2. Think about it—how difficult would it be to write a career book for 'everyone'? Impossible! It would be broad, shallow and boring.
3. If you mistakenly attract the wrong audience to your book, they will be disappointed and leave a poor review.

That's why niching is so important. Choose a reader group you would love to work with and support, then go deep with them in your content. And make it very clear just who they are in your book cover, book content, and in all marketing material.  Book Titles and Big Picture Questions

Let's take a look at five popular books, written by people just like you, and consider what reader dilemma each author has addressed.

*Discover Your Strengths* by Marcus Buckingham
>Reader dilemma: 'I'm not enjoying my career, and I'm feeling lost. I've got no idea what my strengths are, or what I should do next. How can I find out?'

*Girl's Guide to Real Estate* by Donna Lee Brien and Tess Brady
>Reader dilemma: 'Even though I am still young, I'd love to find a way to become more financially secure. How do I do it?'

*Become a Key Person of Influence* by Daniel Priestley.
>Reader dilemma: 'I want to attract more high-paying clients, play on a bigger stage, and have more fun. How do I do that?'

*Making a Living Without a Job* by Barbara Winter
>Reader dilemma: 'How can I make a living doing what I love rather than taking a soul-destroying job?'

*The Purpose Project* by Carolyn Tate
>Reader dilemma: 'I want to be happier in my job and feel my work has purpose. How can I do this?'

# READER RESEARCH

Once you think you know your ideal reader and understand their motivations and problems, it is imperative that you do some research to either verify or disprove this. Writing a book takes time, thought, and determination, so don't wait until after it is published to find out whether or not your assumptions were correct.

If you're writing a book for teenagers, for example, you'd better be ... you guessed it ... talking to teenagers. As you are aware, they see the world very differently to us adults (who usually assume we know best) so set up lots of opportunities for easy conversations with people in your ideal reader group and check those assumptions.

Reader research can be quite informal over a period of time, and based on planned or chance conversations, where you ask questions and note responses.

It can also take the form of surveys with carefully constructed questions that do not lead the respondent, and do give them ample opportunity to express their ideas. Ask what they're anxious about; what they need to know; about their obstacles and their dreams; what they would love to achieve; and what's getting in the way of achieving their goals. Encourage people to be really real and drill down so you can then address true problems in your book.

## MARKET RESEARCH FOR YOUR BOOK

Amazon is a smart place to start because it's still the biggest bookseller on the planet. Look for the bestseller section for non-fiction books similar to the one you wish to write. Open the sample pages to read more information about them, read the reviews and see what's selling, as well as what people like about each individual book.

When you're on Amazon, take note of book titles and sub-titles, which usually offer the key selling point. An effective non-fiction book title will tell people what the book is about, and the sub-title will do a great job of selling the result the book offers the reader.

When Johanna Penn, well-known author and author mentor, wrote a book for authors about selling books, she noticed that the phrase 'How to market a book,' was a popular search term so she named her book accordingly: *How to Market Your Book*. Naturally, it sells very well.

*How to Sell a Book*; *How to Run Like Forrest*; *How to Listen to Your Teenager*: all are powerful frameworks for a book title.

Google Analytics is also another source of frequently-searched keywords. Just as you would use that information in your business marketing material, you can do the same with your book title and/ or sub-title.

Active LinkedIn groups also provide a place for gathering feedback on content ideas and asking questions relevant to the group theme.

Don't forget libraries! They are staffed by trained researchers (called librarians) so if you need help, go to a library, find a trained staff member, and have a really serious talk about how you might best use the library to access information. You might be really surprised by what you can find.

## MAGAZINES

Magazines offer a window into various market segments and industries. If there are any targeting the same audience that you want to reach with your book, you can gather useful information from their media kit, their articles, and the companies paying to advertise there.

You can also find ideas for book titles, sub-titles and content. Oprah's highly successful magazine, O, for example, is full of popular and catchy articles that could be extended into short books. Magazines such as O have the budget and expertise to analyse consumer behaviour very closely, so you can be sure that the article topics, titles and catchy blurbs they use are winners.

# THE BOTTOM LINE

Don't discount the importance of research. You might have in your head at the beginning that you plan to write X, but while doing research, you might expand your ideas to include Y. Or you might scrap X altogether and write a book about Y instead, because the people you've interviewed have told you that X doesn't matter to them at all, but they have a burning passion to discover the intricacies of Y.

—————————

*The following exercise will help you build a clear description of your ideal reader.*

# JOURNAL EXERCISE

## YOUR IDEAL READER

*It's not enough to have a vague sense of your reader, because your reader is looking for something very specific. It might be solace or wisdom, entertainment or escape – but no matter what it is, they are desperate. Why else would they spend hours and hours alone with your work?*

~ Jennie Nash, CEO of Author Accelerator

It is vitally important that you create an ideal reader profile for the book you want to write. Think through these questions:

- *Who wants what you have?*
- *What problems are they struggling with?*
- *What can't they do without your help?*
- *What specifically are they seeking?*
- *What do they need to find out?*
- *Why do you understand them so well?*
- *What can you provide for them?*

For example, if you are writing a cookbook for beginners, put yourself in the shoes (or apron) of an inexperienced cook who wants to improve their skills, make nutritious meals, and save money cooking for their family. Ask yourself, 'How can I give them the information they need in a way that they can easily understand and use?'

Other questions to consider:

*How do I write in a way that inspires them?*

*What level of knowledge and skills do I assume they already have?*

*What can I put in my book (or on my website, linked in my book) to provide them with the tools they need to help them along the way – possibly some worksheets or checklists?*

*How do I make my book relatable, fun, entertaining, inspiring? (What would you love someone to say about your book?)*

*How do I create something they can't put down?*

These are questions you should come back to again and again while writing your book. Think about what you can add that will be of the greatest value to your reader, such as stories, anecdotes, case studies, tools, checklists, links to resources online, and more.

Your book becomes more valuable to others when you help them achieve their own desires.

Spend some time here responding to the questions in the bullet points above.

# BARBARA J. WINTER

*Barbara is a pioneering self-employment advocate, writer and teacher, and resides in California, USA. She is the author of* Making a Living without a Job *and* Winning Ways.

When I began teaching seminars on Making a Living Without a Job in 1988, I thought it would be a short-lived project. It was, after all, a radical notion at the time. Besides I had other topics I wanted to develop. Boy, was I wrong on both counts. I quickly learned that the world was full of people who were looking for alternatives to having a conventional job.

One question kept popping up right from the beginning – 'Do you have a book?' I'd usually mumble some response about planning to have a book in the future. For starters, I wasn't nearly as confident about my writing skills as I was about my speaking skills. I also knew that I did not want to write a book until I had success stories from my students – proof that my ideas worked for others.

After three years of doing my programs in a growing number of adult education centers, I felt ready to tackle a book version. Self-publishing seemed difficult and mysterious, but so did conventional publishing. How was I going to get an agent? Or get a publisher to pay attention?

However, I had decided that I'd love to have a publisher find me, rather than me finding them. I had a seminar coming up in New York and got the crazy idea that some editor would see my program, sign up, and offer me a contract.

That's not exactly what happened. However, when I returned to New York six months later, two publishers sent editors to my seminar. Three days later, they both offered me a contract. My crazy idea had mysteriously worked.

On July 15, 1993, *Making a Living Without a Job* made its debut. It has remained in print ever since. In 2009 it was updated, since the original version did not contain words such as Skype or Internet. However, since my teachings are focused on philosophy and mindset, not the nuts and bolts of self-employment, that framework hasn't changed. The basics have remained the same.

Long ago, I decided I wanted to go for longevity, not be an overnight flash in the pan. My book is only one aspect of that.

Even older is *Winning Ways,* the print newsletter that I began over 30 years ago. I knew that in my own journey, I needed constant reinforcement and suspected I was not alone in that. A print newsletter gets more attention than a digital version. Many of my subscribers, who have been with me for years, say they never throw away an issue and use it as an ongoing resource.

Best of all, it is a vehicle for sharing new ideas and information so it's almost like writing a new book every year.

www.joyfullyjobless.com

# TIME TO PLAN

*If you want to put yourself on the map, publish your own map.*

~ Ashleigh Brilliant

# CHAPTER 5

# YOUR PUBLISHING PROJECT

B ecause you are creating a tangible product that will attract people to you, and will be a valuable asset to your business, take it seriously and map out a plan before you begin. If you don't, chances are your book will become just another discarded dream in the gravel on the edge of life's highway.

I know for sure that my first publishing project, the magazine *Work from Home*, would not have launched in January 1997 without a plan and a definite launch date. Because I was able to secure a distributor for the magazine during the planning stage,

I was given a delivery date; in other words, I committed to supply thousands of copies to the distributor's warehouse in Brisbane by a definite date. External accountability is a powerful motivator.

As a self-publisher you will need to create your own deadlines and accountability, because you won't be dealing with a book distributor immediately. Setting an achievable launch date is a good way to give yourself a target: more on that later in this chapter.

This simple book production diagram on the next page sets out what steps are involved in the publishing process and how long you should allow for them. When done properly, it will provide you with a manageable schedule for completing your project that won't overwhelm you. At the same time, it will motivate you to stay on track and get your book done.

If you decide on a particular launch date for your book before you begin constructing it, work backwards from that date, allowing realistic time frames for each of the steps, and you will soon see that you will need to get into action now.

NOTE: The time frames in the following diagram are guidelines only and every author is unique.

- The editing, design and printing people who work with you on your book will give you their own time requirements, which you must respect.
- Be realistic. A rushed job will cause stress and is more likely to contain mistakes.
- Giving yourself too much time will allow you to wander off your path and even lose interest.

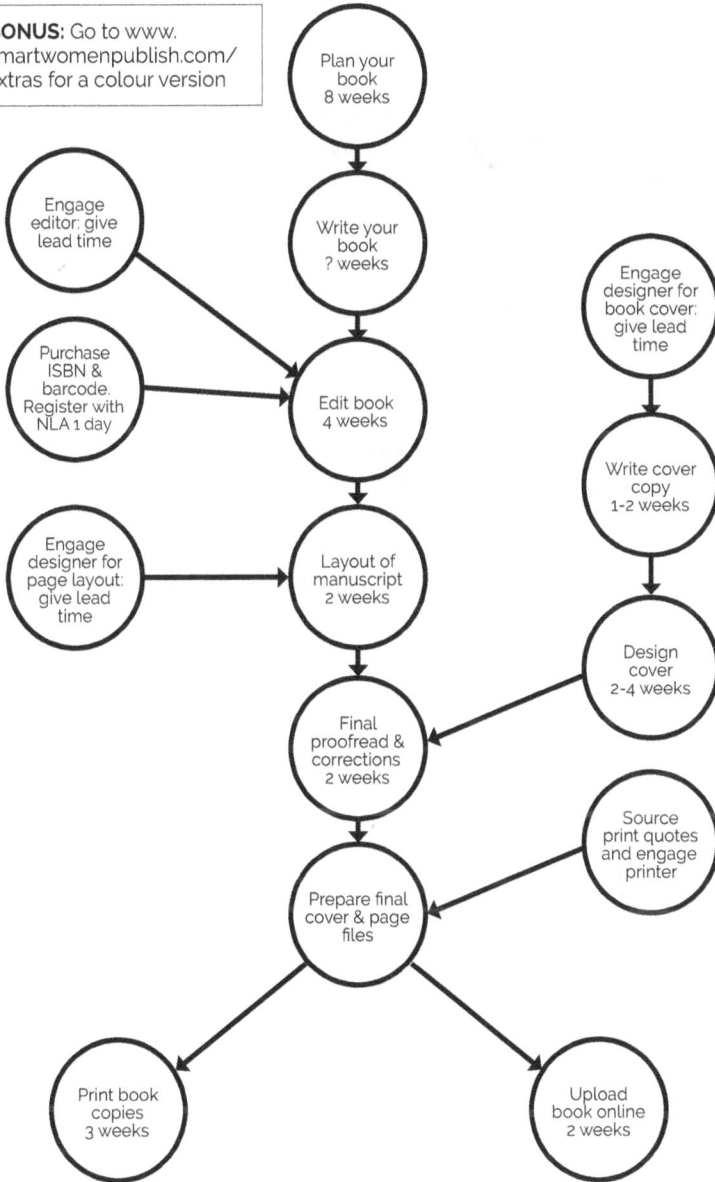

**BONUS:** Go to www.smartwomenpublish.com/extras for a colour version

Plan your book
8 weeks

Engage editor: give lead time

Write your book
? weeks

Engage designer for book cover: give lead time

Purchase ISBN & barcode. Register with NLA 1 day

Edit book
4 weeks

Write cover copy
1-2 weeks

Engage designer for page layout: give lead time

Layout of manuscript
2 weeks

Design cover
2-4 weeks

Final proofread & corrections
2 weeks

Source print quotes and engage printer

Prepare final cover & page files

Print book copies
3 weeks

Upload book online
2 weeks

———————

*Referring to the Publishing Flow diagram in this chapter, and the following exercise, build your own publishing timeline in these pages or in your book journal.*

# JOURNAL EXERCISE

## TIMELINE

Plan out the first draft of your publishing schedule here, or in your own book journal.

**STAGE 1: PLAN**

Allow 8 to 12 weeks in order to plan your book thoroughly and do market research.

PLAN from _____ to _____

**STAGE 2: WRITE**

**Depending on your availability,** allow from 6 weeks upwards to 26 weeks to write your book. Don't allow yourself too long because you will lose your momentum, but be realistic. Ideas need time to seed and grow. Give yourself a deadline and identify how you will be most productive. Set aside regular time every day/weekend/week/month.

PRODUCE from _____ to _____

## STAGE 3: PUBLISH

**Substantive edit:** Allow at least 4 weeks from commencement – add any extra time you may be on the editor's wait list.

**Design:**

**Cover –** Gather cover ideas as you write, and begin your cover design during the editing stage. Allow 4 weeks.

**Pages –** Allow 4 weeks for comfort and low stress while pages are designed, checked, updated, checked, updated some more, and proofread thoroughly (more than once).

**Print:** Allow 3 weeks from completion of book layout, which gives you time to check a print proof copy properly before approving a larger print run.

**Online distribution:** Allow 2 weeks from final approval of book layout to create your e-book files and upload to Amazon and other book sellers.

PUBLISH from _____ to _____

## STAGE 4: LAUNCH & MARKET

**Launch:** Allow another two weeks after you receive your print books AND your books are available online to go public with several launch events, both live and online.

**Market:** This is an ongoing process over several years – not a crazy stressful rush in the first few months.

EXPECTED LAUNCH period commences _____

## BEGIN WORK ON THE BOOK

Now, looking at these dates, when do you need to begin work on your book? Write the date here: _____

**BONUS:** Go to www.smartwomenpublish.com/extras to download your Book Deadlines planner. Fill it out, and place in on your wall in full view so you feel accountable to those dates.

# KATHRYN HODGES

*Kathryn is a lawyer and principal of her own practice, Integrated Family Law, on the Sunshine Coast in Queensland. She is the author of* Who Gets the Dog? A real conversation about separation, divorce and finding your happiness again.

My biggest challenge as a self-publisher was turning my word collection into a useful book for separating couples. I definitely would have struggled to create a lovely looking, and therefore comforting, book for my readers without guidance. I simply would not have been able to create and publish my book on my own as I had no idea about the practical elements involved, and had no idea where to turn to get help with editing, layout, cover art, ISBN information, etc.

Since publishing, I believe that my book has helped people who approach me for legal advice to feel comforted that I know what I talk about, and they can trust my guidance and advice. I feel like I don't have to answer many 'why should I choose you' questions anymore, as my book answers them for me.

My book has also helped to define the type of work that I do best for clients by giving them a lot of what is in my head (and my heart) up front. This helps me to find and keep clients who are aligned with my ways of working and supporting people through their legal issues.

I have received emails, usually late at night, from readers saying, 'I have just been reading your book, and it's not just me feeling like this, is it?' When I read those emails, I feel so very grateful that I pushed through my discomfort and got help, so that my book was created and can help people feel less alone and lost during their separation. I did not expect that feeling to be so deeply nourishing for me.

I have also been surprised, and often find myself having a little knowing smile, when I receive other emails saying, 'I've just realised I have been doing it all wrong, haven't I? There's probably an easier way.' Those moments remind me of the ripples of change that the choices of just one person can make.

I am deeply grateful for Bev's kind and strong support helping others like me to get our books out into the world. Just imagine the ripples of change she is creating that way.

www.integratedfamilylaw.com.au

*A quantum leap, by definition, means moving into unchartered territory with no guide to follow. You personally draw the map as you go.*

~ Price Pritchett, in *you2*

## CHAPTER 6

# YOUR BOOK PLANS

L et's face it; you can start a business without a 50-page micro-detailed business plan. But you would not even step onto that path without desire, vision and enthusiasm – and at least a basic breakdown of the key elements involved: product/service; consumer trends; target market; competition; skills analysis; financials; marketing methods, and more.

You can also write a book without a 50-page detailed book business plan, but you will be very wise to take the time to create a version that steps you through some serious thinking before sitting down to create your first book draft. Otherwise you may complete and launch your book, only to realise you have missed opportunities and perhaps even written the wrong book for your business.

## YOUR BOOK BUSINESS PLAN

Preparing a book plan provides a structure for gaining clarity about the important aspects of your book. Because you are creating a new product for your business that you intend to use for leverage, and investing time and money in the process, it is critical that you work through the key elements and prepare a thorough document that confirms you are on the right track.

This plan is also a very useful document to have on hand if or when you approach others to be involved in your book in some way – as collaborators, contributors, investors, sponsors, etc.

Your book business plan will include:

- Working title and sub-title
- Why you are writing this book
- About this book
- What makes this book unique
- Target audience
- Why they will read this book
- Target readership research results
- Author credibility
- Draft contents page
- Back cover blurb

- Proposed length
- Author following
- Marketing and promotion ideas
- Production timeline
- Financials

BONUS: to download the full framework for your Book Business Plan as a PDF, with instructions, go to www.smartwomenpublish.com/extras

# THE BENEFITS OF A BOOK BUSINESS PLAN

You gain clarity on why you are in business, where you want your book to take you, and who you want to serve and support in the future.

You gain clarity on the main message of your book.

You define who your ideal reader is, and get an idea of the size of your target market segment through good research. Use sources such as The Australian Bureau of Statistics (ABS); state government departments; local councils; industry bodies; professional membership organisations; libraries/librarians; research groups; online research; universities; etc.

You find out what your reader *really* wants, rather than what you think they want.

You define your point of difference. (Rohit Bhargava, for example, found the point of difference for his book *Personality Not Included: Why Companies Lose Their Authenticity–And How Great Brands get It Back* by positioning it between books about business and books about marketing.)

You find ways to give your readers compelling reasons to buy your book. It can be something really simple or quite complex, but you need to identify it.

You set out a production schedule for your book.

You figure out what skills you have – and where you will need help.

You put thought into your existing audience and how to build connections while you write your book, in preparation for marketing.

You are prepared and professional when you have an opportunity to pitch your book, if someone unexpectedly says, 'I've got a friend who's a literary agent. Why don't you send her a synopsis of the book? She may be able to bring your work to the attention of a publishing house.'

You also think about the money equation, and if you want to pitch for funding, sponsorships or partnerships, a book plan shows you are serious and prepared. Who would want to risk their money or reputation with someone who does not take their own work seriously? (I cover funding in Chapter 11, expected costs in Chapter 12, and ways to leverage your book in Part D.)

# BEWARE THE LIZARD BRAIN

As you set out on this writing journey, your lizard brain (as Seth Godin calls it) will kick into action the closer you get to purposeful action. You know it is doing its job when you become aware of these thoughts:

*What have I got to say that is different?*

*Who am I to write a book?*

*Somebody else has said everything I want to say, so it seems like I have nothing more to contribute.*

You may well be thinking that right now.

The 'lizard', as you probably know, is your amygdala, an almond-shaped section of the limbic system located in the temporal lobe of your brain, and its job is to protect you. It senses change and can overrule your logic with a warning that you may be in danger. Crazy lizard!

You may become aware of a fear of not measuring up. A fear of not having enough clout to write a book. Or of feeling like an imposter.

Your familiar, faded and worn limiting beliefs may be mixed in there too, telling you that an author you are not.

A simple way to nudge this negative feeling is to write a powerful and affirming phrase like this: 'This book is about the world of self-publishing business books for beginners, according to Bev Ryan.'

Other examples:

*This book is the world of mature women seeking career change according to Jill.*

Or *This book is the world of home cooking for large families according to Tania.*

That little phrase instantly gives you permission to put your unique voice into your book and helps you realise that you don't have to cover everything that's ever been covered in the history of the world on your topic: you can write about a microcosm or address a very specific niche market.

———————————

*Complete the following exercise in these pages or in your book journal, and prepare a powerful statement about your book that will remind you that your work is important.*

# JOURNAL EXERCISE

## SYNOPSIS

It's your turn! Fill in the blanks and place it where it will remind you constantly:

*'My book will be for (your ideal audience)* _____

_____

_____

*who need (the process and/or result you can provide)* _____

_____

because they are currently struggling with *(their problem*_____

- - - - - - - - - - - - - - - - - - - - - - - - - - - - - - - - - -

- - - - - - - - - - - - - - - - - - - - - - - - - - - - - - - - - -

_____

*My book will therefore be about (your book topic)* _____

_____

_____

*according to (your name)* _____

_____

*and I promise my readers that (your promise to your reader that you will ensure your book will fulfill as you write it)* _____

_____

_____

Use the following blank pages to practise this until you are happy with what you write.

Once you have prepared a clear and strong synopsis, you might like to replicate it in a poster for your office wall, to remind you of your promise.

_____

# CHRISTINE FRANKLIN

---

*Christine is a psychologist, based in North Queensland, who is passionate about rural health and its role in the vitality and sustainability of remote communities. She is the author of* The Extra Mile: The Essential Guide for Health Professionals Going Bush.

My book provides strategies for health professionals choosing to move to a rural or remote workplace, and provides information and guidance relevant to living and working remotely, to help them cope with the transition.

Mentally, the most difficult aspects of writing the book were identifying myself as 'an author' and having the confidence to believe that I had something worthwhile to share – and that others might be prepared to purchase that knowledge. From a practical point of view, finding the time to sit and write in an already very busy life was challenging. This was only solved when I began rising at 4am and created an extra two hours in my day. I also had no idea about the logistics of publishing and what steps to take, in what order, and what help existed. Having Bev Ryan as a book coach was essential to this process.

Just having published the book gave me a tremendous sense of achievement and satisfaction; it almost did not matter if anyone

---

else read it. Writing and publishing took enormous commitment, focus and personal sacrifice, so aside from being relieved to have reached the finish line I was also just a little bit proud of myself for going the distance.

The book now gives me greater confidence to sell my message (and myself). It's like a talking business card that endures – people don't throw out books. It has led to invitations to speak at events and conferences, and gives me greater credibility. It's not that I suddenly know more about the subject matter than I did before I wrote the book – it's just that people have begun acknowledging that expertise and engaging me on different levels. I have even been invited to speak at a Senate enquiry.

An unexpected benefit of publishing? I am now a morning person and my days are way more productive!

www.sybellahealth.com.au

*Every great building once begun as a building plan. That means, sitting in that building plan on the table is a mighty structure not yet seen. It is the same with dreams.*

~ Israelmore Ayivor,
author of *Shaping The Dream*

## CHAPTER 7

# YOUR BOOK CONTENT PLAN

More planning! Some of you will love this stage because it is creative and allows you to dream big. It also gives you fertile ground for procrastination, so there will come a time when you have to make a decision about the plan and begin writing.

Fortunately a book in progress is a very pliable object, so if, as you write, you realise the plan needs adjustment, go ahead and course correct. (In fact, some things will only become clear as you write: for example, I have just separated what was Chapter 6 in the first plan for this book into Chapters 6 and 7.)

## STARTING POINT

Once you've formed a clear picture of who your reader is, it is also important to have a clear understanding of their ambitions, highest hopes, and aspirations. You must then offer what they really need from you in order to fulfil them.

The promise of your book should be information, solutions, fresh insights or inspiration, which attract your target reader to your pages.

Start your book where your reader is; consider where you want your reader to be when they have finished reading it; and construct a way of taking them there. What logical, enjoyable and hopeful journey will you take them on?

Once you have defined that, you will have clarity and direction and can decide what material you will be covering, as well as the actual structure of your book.

Then sit with the concept of your book and spend some time thinking about how you move your book out of the 'it's been done before' zone and into the 'interesting' zone.

- Can you write a book for a niche market that you understand, rather than a broader one?

- Can you combine various ideas and concepts and come up with something fresh?
- Can you combine or include work by other people who have expertise in an area that is complementary to yours?
- Can you add a well-known individual into a chapter to add value, credibility and diversity to the book?

During this planning stage, consider creating one or more informal, relaxed focus groups. Invite people you can trust to give useful feedback and input, and who are from your target readership group. Toss around some ideas. Ask them – perhaps over a good bottle of wine – to think about what you can add to your book that is going to make it really interesting for your target reader. Ask how you can add a WOW factor in there. Ask your focus group what they'd want to read if they were reading your book.

Just be careful not to go too crazy with your content. If you go too far, you risk readers thinking, 'This is too weird!' – and that is certainly not what you want.

## A BOOK I LOVE

*Steal Like An Artist* by American Austin Kleon is a small, thought-provoking book broken up into ten chapters about being creative and sharing your art (or work) with the world. His book became a *New York Times* bestseller very quickly, and it's easy to see why. Put simply, it's a simple book for people who consciously aim to live a life rich with purpose.

The messages throughout it will inspire you as you write your own book. For example, Chapter Two states, 'Don't wait until you know who you are to get started'.

Some of his other key messages that apply to you right now are:

- Write the book you want to read.
- Do good work and share it with people.
- Be nice: the world is a small town.
- Be boring. It's the only way to get work done.
- Creativity is subtraction.

## CRAFTING YOUR MESSAGE

You may already have a very clear idea of what you want to write, or you may still be a bit fuzzy about what your book is going to look like. Here are some simple formats that may work for you:

- A personal story or a shared experience written in first person: 'I did this and I did that; I learnt this and I learnt that.' (If that is all you wish to write, think of that as a memoir.)
- The 'how to' format is very useful and has wide appeal because it speaks directly to the reader and shows them the solution to their problem. You might not use the words 'How to' in the title, but that concept provides a logical structure for your book.
- A collaborative book allows other people to add their voices to your book. You coordinate the other writers and give them clear guidelines to ensure you receive useful and relevant content.

- You might write an industry-specific book, and could use the 'how to' format or collaborative approach. For example, rather than 'How to start a business,' you might produce 'How to start a hairdressing business'. Or 'Ten sports coaches tell you how to build a winning team'.
- You'll find a big market for books about spiritual wellness, mind-body-soul, or new age content – but be careful that you are not re-hashing others' well-worn material. You have to find your unique approach.
- The popularity of short inspirational books is also a good reminder that books don't have to be long-winded.

# WHAT TYPE OF BOOK WILL YOU WRITE?

**Instructional:** Most business owner-authors prefer this option because it allows for logical content that shows steps or processes, and their preferred readers are likely to be looking to ease a situation in some way or another. You can add supporting material to enhance your content, such as stories, case studies, diagrams, tables, lists, etc.

Here are some examples:

- *Smart Women Publish* – a step-by step guide to self-publishing
- *Made to Stick* – how to attract sales and buzz for your business
- *Write It Down, Make It Happen* – how to get what you want
- *How to Win Friends & Influence People*
- *How to Draw Cool Stuff*

**TIP:** You could use a draft title of 'How to xxxx' to guide you in structuring and writing the book, then drop off the 'how to' from the title later. Some examples: *Become a Highly Paid Speaker and Publish a Business Book.*

**Persuasive:** Some call this model 'thought leadership'. You write your insightful opinion of an issue, based on evidence, hoping to influence readers' opinions. A well-written book with a fresh viewpoint can give you traction, such as *The 4-Hour Work Week* by Tim Ferris, but the format requires writing skill AND a new and unusual idea. Do not present hackneyed material, or it will backfire.

Other examples include:

- *Freakonomics* – an economist presents a rogue theory about economic incentive
- *Quiet* – a book about the power of being an introvert in a noisy world
- *The Life-Changing Magic of Tidying Up* – a theory for cleaning house based on the concept of joy

**List:** This style of book can be a way to get started. Andrew Griffith, Australia's foremost small business authority, found his feet as an author with *101 Ways to Market Your Business* and has gone on to write seven more '101 Ways' books, as well as several other non-fiction titles. The format is simple, content can be segmented into different sub-topics, and you could even supplement your original content with others' credited contributions as well, to get underway.

Some examples:

- *The 7 Habits of Highly Effective People*
- *The Top Five Regrets of the Dying*
- *The 5 Love Languages*
- *Top Secret Restaurant Recipes*
- *It! 9 Secrets of the Rich and Famous*

**Narrative:** You largely tell your own experience of a specific topic, with lessons learned, with the intention of informing/guiding others.

- *Eat, Pray, Love* by Elizabeth Gilbert – a memoir of one woman's journey to find herself
- *Becoming* by Michelle Obama – a memoir that inspires women to defy expectations
- *The Girl Who Smiled Beads* by Clementine Wamariya – the harsh reality of the life of a refugee
- *Tomorrow Will be Different* by Sarah McBride – this book sheds light on the constant struggle for LGBTQ+ rights and inclusion

**Compilation:** By sharing authorship you may dilute the impact of the book, but there are some very successful books that refute that, for example the 'Chicken Soup' series with Jack Canfield. You can invite others to share their views and experience with you in your book, by contributing around the central theme. These views may conflict with your own, support your own, or add a perspective you do not have. You may become the curator of others' knowledge and simply gather content from various sources, then present it with or without your commentary. You can co-publish with others whose skills and experience complement yours but do not overlap, though it is important in this case to ensure you are writing for the same audience.

- *Cattlemen in Pearls* – a collection of profiles of women in the beef industry in Australia
- *Cherished* – a collection of stories about cherished pets by Barbara Abercrombie and other authors
- *InFertility* – secrets, struggles and successes by Colleen Reagan Noon and other authors

**Hybrid:** This book type combines elements from two formats, often 'instructional' information combined with the traditional structure of a 'chronological narrative'. Decide on your main intention or purpose, and categorise your book that way – memoir or how-to, for example – but combine both structures to achieve this.

Here are perfect examples:

- *Real Happiness* by Sharon Salzberg – how to adopt habits to make you happier, combined with the author's story of working on these habits in her own life.
- *Bird by Bird* by Anne Lamott – stories about her writing life, to provide distinct lessons learned. It reads like a memoir, but it is categorised as 'how-to' because the author's intention is to show others how to live the life of a writer.

## DECIDING ON STEPS

It's important to break your book up into chapters and outline the steps readers will take on their journey. For example, a cook writing a book for people who have never cooked before would ask themselves, 'How do I help my inexperienced reader to become a confident cook?'

What does your reader need to know first; what does she need to know second; what does she need to know next? These questions will become your chapters, and the title of each chapter should reflect the step that chapter will help your reader to take.

## QUESTIONS TO ASK YOURSELF AND OTHERS

While you are breaking your book down into steps, it is also crucial that you keep a focus on the big questions as you write. *Who are the people that want to read this book, and where are they in their life? How can I structure this book so that it has the most impact?*

When readers pick up your book, flip it over and read the back cover, you want them to think, 'Wow, super interesting. I have to buy this book – it is speaking to me!'

## PLANNING YOUR CONTENT

I am sure you remember writing essays at school with this simple format – introduction, body, conclusion. You wrote the body first, then added the introduction and conclusion later.

It should be no surprise that your book will have the same arrangement – after all, that is what our brains make sense of. Of course you can mix it up and take a new approach, but you run the risk of losing your audience if they are looking for logical content they can easily absorb and implement.

# SAMPLE BOOK STRUCTURE

The title of this book, mentioned earlier in Chapter 4, tells us exactly what it offers: *I Don't Know What I Want, But I Know It's Not This: A Step-by-Step Guide to Finding Gratifying Work* by Julie Hansen.

Its table of contents clearly illuminates the reader's journey through the book:

> *Part One: Where Are You Now?*
> *Part Two: Where Do You Want to Be?*
> *Part Three: How Do You Get There?*

Each of those sections then contains several well-titled chapters to create an uncomplicated and simply defined structure for her book. The reader can see exactly what they will get when they dive into the book, and Part Three offers clear solutions (a step-by-step guide) to a widely held problem – career dissatisfaction.

## YOUR CONTENT

### Your book structure

Keeping in mind that you are taking your readers on a journey, write a list of the high-level steps or points they need to follow, work through or understand in order to get from where they are now to where they want to be. Do a brain dump and write them in any order.

Then rearrange these key points in the most logical order and they become the first rough plan for your book content. You will definitely refine this list over time: you will probably get rid of some because you realise you do not need to include everything you know; and you may add something as you write that you then see as essential.

The journal exercise at the end of this chapter will help you to begin planning the breakdown of the content for your book in more detail. The goal here is to get clear on the key concepts in your chapters in your book, and the order in which these concepts will be best presented and understood.

## FRONT MATTER

Just when you think you have written your book you will remember (or your editor will remind you) that there are sections in the front and back of your book that require time, focus, and words. More words.

You will choose to use some or all of the following front matter sections: think about what the reader needs to know or understand at the outset of the book so their journey through the book is clear.

**Title page**: A basic black-and-white first page, usually based on the cover design.

**Imprint page**: All the copyright and legal information relating to your book, including disclaimer. This includes ISBN and National

Library of Australia registration statement. Obtain ISBN and barcode for the back cover here: www.myidentifers.com.au

Register your book with the National Library of Australia here: www. nla.gov.au/cip.

**Endorsements/testimonials** *(optional)*: This includes advance praise from reviewers, which will typically appear in the book before or after the title page – or in the back if you prefer.

**Dedication** *(optional)*: A few words dedicating the book to a particular person or to special people – usually just a line or two.

**Acknowledgements** *(optional)*: Usually a few paragraphs in the front or back section, stating appreciation for particular people who assist or support you.

**Table of contents**: At the submission to editor stage, do not include page numbers because these will change when the book is typeset.

**Foreword** *(optional)*: Written by someone other than you, preferably a notable person who will give your book credibility.

**Preface** *(optional)*: Written by you, explaining why you came to write the book.

**Introduction** *(optional)*: Also written by you, outlining what readers can expect to find in the book.

**How to use this book** *(optional)*: This section is useful if you have written a handbook or a book containing sections, actions and/or exercises which require some explanation.

# END MATTER

In the back of the book, after the manuscript, you can add extra information such as:

**Call-to-action page**: Think of this as an advertisement. This is where you list your contact details and a clear, easy invitation to partake in an offer or other action. You can add other marketing information but keep it simple and easy to do.

**About the author**: An interesting piece about yourself, which gives more context to your work, and allows the reader to get to know you better. This should be succinct, interesting and informative, and can be placed in the front or back of the book.

**References or Endnotes** *(if required)*: A list of sources you have referred to directly through your book. These should be numbered and matched to superscript numbering throughout the text in your book. We suggest you add this information in the back of the book rather than as page footnotes, for ease of layout.

**Bibliography** *(if required)*: A list of other material you have accessed while researching content of this book, that is not referenced directly.

**Resources** *(optional)*: You might want to add other things you know will be of value to your reader.

**Epilogue** *(optional)*: The final segment of a story and effectively serves as one final chapter.

**Afterword** *(optional)*: A statement on the entire narrative, and it is frequently told from a different perspective, as is the Foreword.

**Appendix** *(optional)*: Contains information that is not essential within the book, but supports your information or validates your conclusions.

**Index** *(if required)*: This can be created using index software (simple version) or by engaging an indexer for a more complex cross-referenced version.

## ADDITIONAL CONTENT

This step is critical if you want your book to grow your business. If your goal is to benefit from book sales alone, you are missing the most lucrative and valuable part of the business book equation.

It is vital that you grow your own list or database of people interested in your book. If you sell and distribute your book from your website alone, and collect every purchaser's details, including email address, you will achieve that goal when you add that contact information to your list.

However, if your book is also – or only – available on Amazon or another online distributor's site, you will have no idea who your readers are.

Make sure you insert some instructions, or an offer, in your book which will invite readers to go to your website to gather additional helpful, relevant and attractive material or resources you have prepared earlier. In doing so, ask them to join your mailing list so you can provide even more useful things. Work with your book designer to ensure all bonus material you offer is top quality.

You can also offer free 20-minute consultation calls this way, using a booking calendar on your website. Or access to free recorded webinars and other digital content.

―――――――――

*In the next exercise, you will write your first piece of marketing copy for your book, and begin plotting your chapter topics.*

# JOURNAL EXERCISE

## TAKING SHAPE

Check out the power of these two small words: 'You too'. This is a very effective way to convey value to the reader while making the material you present immediately relevant.

**EXERCISE A:**

When it is put together with your book's overall concept, this little phrase is something you can use in your marketing efforts. You can use it on the back cover of your book, and you can use it on your website to tell people about your book. If you have marketing experience, you have probably come across it before.

Here's the format:

*You too can* _____

*so that* _____

*even though* _____

As an example, you could use this to promote a cookbook for beginners:

*You too can produce easy and tasty meals for your family so that they think you are Super-Mum, even though right now you might feel like a total flop in the kitchen.*

The statement reassures that change is possible. You can see why this is much more effective than saying, 'Here's a book with fantastic recipes that everyone needs to know'.

**EXERCISE B:**

What type of book will you write, and why? (Refer to pages 131-134.)

------------------------------------------------------------------------

------------------------------------------------------------------------

**EXERCISE C:**

What is the overall shape of the journey you are taking your reader on? What do they have to do or learn to get the power or prize or understanding they are seeking, according to your methods and philosophies?

In the following blank pages, or your book journal, map out the steps you will take your reader through to move them from PAIN to POWER.

# TANYA BARTOLINI

*Tanya is an Australian entrepreneur now living in California, USA. Her decision to publish her cookbook* Blending the Cultures *dramatically changed her life.*

Growing up in an Italian family in North Queensland, food has always been a passion of mine and a huge part of my life. It wasn't something that I initially thought others would be interested in reading about, so when I decided to write a food and culture book I struggled with self-doubt. I also had no idea how to begin writing a book, so book coaching sessions with Bev Ryan helped me get started.

I am so glad I did: the book completely changed my life. I paused my career in finance and was launched into the wonderful world of food. Suddenly I went from speaking with financial advisers to cooking on the Today show and ABC radio. Every day I got to talk about my passion and also influence others to do the same. So not only do I feel that the book was pivotal for me, but also for others who heard my story or read my book and could relate, and thought 'I want to take the leap and do something different or make a change in my life'.

Publishing a book automatically gives you credibility. I would have never been given the opportunity to appear on television or radio, or even get the social media following I did, if not for the fact that I published a book. I didn't quite understand that at first, but I know that publishing a book gave me credibility in an area completely removed from my experience and qualifications in the finance industry.

Footnote: *Tanya's success sparked a fire in her husband too. They now reside in California with their children and continue to take on new challenges and follow their entrepreneurial dreams after building Jacobi, a new financial technology company, headquartered in San Francisco.*

www.jacobistrategies.com

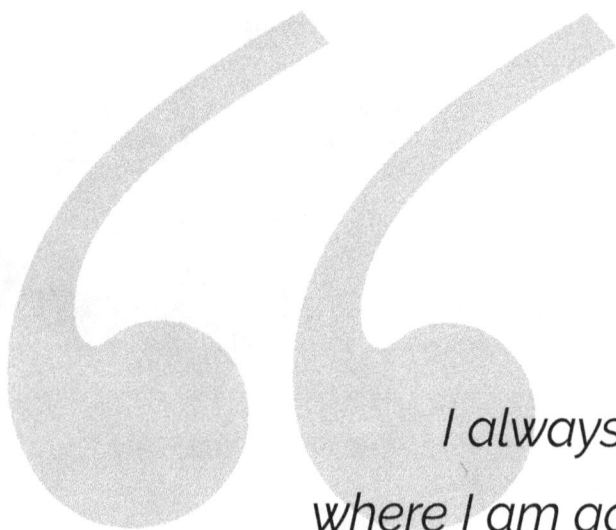

*I always get to where I am going by walking away from where I have been.*

~ Winnie the Pooh

## CHAPTER 8

# YOUR SUPPORT TEAM

T he idea of writing and publishing a book has excited countless people for centuries. The word 'author' means many things to many people, and early in this book you will have identified what it means to you.

A word of warning though: writing is a solitary activity and requires vision, determination and resilience. Think about how you have achieved major goals in the past: if you are the type of person who needs support and interaction to re-energise yourself when you are flagging, you will need to find ways to create a support team to see you through the book writing stage.

If, however, you love to hide away and work with ideas and words, you will find the writing stage a pleasure, but may struggle with the creative aspects of bringing those words into a tangible product.

# TALENT PROFILING

I have trained as a consultant using the Talent Dynamics profiling model (based on Roger Hamilton's Wealth Dynamics model) and find it to be a useful tool when coaching clients through their book production stages. It is a simple way of looking at people's natural strengths, where they will flourish, and also where they may need to reach out to others for support in the process.

Here is a simple summary of four of the key profiles – and there are eight in total: you will probably see yourself clearly in one of these, although most of us are a mix of a dominant trait and secondary traits.

**Creator:** If you are creative and outgoing, you will enjoy coming up with book ideas and planning the content. When it comes to the design phase you will enjoy the visual elements taking shape, although you will need to listen to the professionals – you may not always have the best ideas, and the book is about the reader, not you. A good designer knows that and can direct you.

As a creator, you will also confidently speak about your book and your greater vision when it is time to promote it.

You may however struggle with the writing stage, as this requires you to work alone for long periods of time. You may decide to reach out for assistance and engage a ghost writer to help bring it home after you establish the content structure and key messages.

You may also be quick to assume you know exactly what your readers want, rather than slow things down and put extra time into research and conversation, where you listen to others' needs and see things from their perspective.

**Supporter:** Your preferred activity is to support others and help them shine, so the idea of becoming an author with the spotlight firmly on you can be quite daunting.

Remember why you are so valuable to others though – it is because you are very good at what you do, you have a breadth of skills, and you are very tuned into others' needs and problems. Which is what an author must be. You will also be very adept at making this book happen, because that is what you do best, and you will enjoy working collaboratively with the production team.

You may struggle with giving yourself permission to put yourself first when you are writing the book, so take time out to do just that. You may also be uncomfortable speaking up about your book and going public when it is released, but remember to speak from and to the heart and you will be fine. That is your greatest asset.

**Trader:** You love providing great customer service and want to give people what they want. You enjoy market research, and you are able to see things from others' perspectives. You are also skilled at managing projects by bringing people and processes together to deliver results on time and as promised. You enjoy buying and selling, and have an objective view of the world.

You will enjoy researching and planning your book so that it solves specific problems, and you will find the solitude of writing and the logic of the production stage very enjoyable. You will however need to trust your editor and designer, who may want to add a little more personality or individual difference to your book.

**Lord:** (I quickly add that this is not my preferred term – it is the term coined by the founder of this profiling tool.) You are risk-averse and like to see proof in numbers, rather than act on a hunch or intuition. You are happy to do the legwork required to establish that a project is viable before you begin. You love certainty and usually prefer to work alone. Your greatest strengths are analytical skills, risk aversion and need for control.

You will create a very thorough book plan (including the financials) and will proceed if you feel it is warranted. Your manuscript will be well-researched and will contain supportive numbers and details, but it may be quite dry reading for some – although it will be logical and will provide solutions to problems. You may struggle to resist micro-managing in the production stage, so this is where you need to step back and trust other professionals to do what they are best at – editing and designing.

> **Note:** You can access the Talent Dynamics Profile Test here: www.talent-dynamics.com/profile-test/. Contact me if you would like to discuss your results in relation to publishing.

# TEAM SUPPORT

Many people dream of achieving big goals; a percentage of those will begin, but quite a low number will actually see the process through to fruition. As I struggled to bring my first idea for a magazine to life all those years ago, I was struck by the truth in these words by Barbara Sher in her book *Wishcraft–How To Get What You Really Want*:

*Isolation is the dream killer.*

How true is that! So what can you do about it?

You can create your own support team, mastermind group or accountability group locally or online, or join an existing one, and focus on achieving your unique goals with team support and access to resources, collective knowledge, connections and energy, while at the same time helping others achieve their goals.

Naturally, other group members must be positive and uplifting, have commitment to a goal, as well as proven ability, and be willing to give as much support as they receive.

Google is a useful source if you want to know more about Barbara Sher's concept of success teams or other types of mastermind groups. They are simple and effective, if run well, and you can easily create something similar. You could set up your own 'book team' by finding others like yourself who also need accountability and support, or contact me for assistance.

# THE PROFESSIONALS

To produce a quality book that will be taken seriously in the business world, and that reflects your own high standards, it is imperative that you use professionals who specialise in working with non-fiction books for these functions: editing, book cover design, page layout, and printing. Chapter 12 contains more information.

# PUBLISHING OPTIONS

### Self-publish

As a DIY self-publisher you manage every step of the process: find your way through the publishing maze; write your content; source your own editing, design and print experts as you need them, and trust they know what they are doing; upload your book for online distribution; launch and market your book … all while making a living at the same time.

### Publishing service providers

One-stop publishing services provide you with a project manager skilled in bringing quality publications to life, and they become your one point of contact as they manage the production for you. They have their own team of tried and true professionals with expertise in editing, cover design, page layout, printing and online distribution. They make also offer extra services such as ghost writing, author websites, marketing collateral design and more, through associates.

---

You simply pay for services rendered, and once your book is produced, you own every aspect of your book, have full access to all accounts set up in your name, and retain all profits from sales.

*(See the final page in this book for information about the author's publishing service for non-fiction writers.)*

### Hybrid option

This can sometimes sound like a traditional publishing company because they 'publish' your book for you under their label, but they do ask you to contribute to the costs yourself, and they provide a supply of books to you. Once published, they also take a percentage of sales because they assist with marketing. However, you must still drive sales yourself, so check this option carefully before proceeding.

Ask who owns the ISBN for your book; what rights you have to re-use your own content; what access you have to online distribution accounts such as Amazon and IngramSpark; what percentage of sales they take; what marketing processes they guarantee to implement and for how long.

If they suddenly close up shop (which happens) what happens to your book? (I recently had to rescue a book for a client after their 'publisher' closed down.)

### Traditional publishers

A publishing company enters what is basically a business contract with an author if they feel they will profit from investing resources into publishing and marketing the author's work. The publisher buys the right to publish a book and pays the author royalties from sales. They fund editing, design, printing, distribution and marketing.

The downsides are loss of control of your book, a lengthy wait for the publishing process to take place, and marketing support that may seem to be insufficient, haphazard or brief.

As the author, you are still expected to energetically market your own book, and ideally bring a strong existing following, good connections, and a marketable personal brand to the arrangement.

As a non-fiction writer, you can either find a literary agent to represent you, or send a submission directly to publishers who make that option available on their website. You must identify the right category for your book, and you will need to submit a query letter plus book proposal, with several sample chapters, and a synopsis of each chapter.

––––––––––––––

*In the next exercise, gather your thoughts on the support you will need as you write and publish your book.*

# JOURNAL EXERCISE

## SUPPORT

Make some notes about the sources of support you can access to assist you.

- What skills, experience and knowledge do you already have that will be a bonus when preparing and publishing your own book?
- Who do you have around you that you can rely on to be a positive support? In what way?
- Identify anyone who may bring you down or dampen your enthusiasm. You do not have to share your book dream with them, because you do not need negativity.
- How could you create your own accountability group to help you stay on track and reach your goals?
- Which publishing option appeals to you at this stage?

# JANE GRIEVE

*Jane is a storyteller, freelance writer, and business owner in Dalby, Queensland. She has authored two books –* Slippin' on the Lino *and* In Stockmen's Footsteps.

To forge a new pathway for oneself in unknown territory is always difficult. I didn't know where to begin, when I committed to self-publishing 'a book' for a group of women friends (calling ourselves '9 Ante Portas') who decided to pursue our artistic dreams for an art show to be held on a specific date in 10 months' time. Writing a book for a book's sake is a nebulous article indeed!

My situation was possibly unusual in that I had a deadline (Brisbane Show Week, August 2009) and I had a reason (because I was part of a group who had declared that each of us was to produce something according to our artistic bent) but I didn't have a subject! All I knew was that I wanted to be the author of a book, simply because I'd always dreamed of being one, not because I felt strongly about any one subject.

Once enough of the prescribed 10 months had elapsed to put me into a total panic about my so-called book, every aspect from my decision about what to write, to coming face-to-face with the finished book, was difficult.

Believing in myself and my skill as a writer was one of the most difficult hurdles. My friend Chrissie, part of the original group, who has sadly since passed, nursed me daily through my uncertainty.

The actual book, when completed, changed my perception of myself as a writer; it changed other peoples' perception of me as a writer.

The fact of its existence in published form was a pathway to my credibility as both a writer and a speaker. I was invited to speak at various forums. The fact that the book was based on humour meant that I was perceived as a funny person, which is a very positive vibe and one that I carried with a lot of enjoyment.

I marketed my book and as it was short stories, I saw an opening in recording them for radio – which I did. The regional ABC took them up and played them weekly, which expanded my profile hugely. An unexpected indirect benefit of self-publishing was then an invitation to write my memoir, from Allen & Unwin publishers. It was manna from heaven and the pinnacle of my dream.

Serendipity has literally paved my way. It brought Bev Ryan to my door (or me to hers, actually); it had me greet my to-be 9 Ante Portas friends, as I emerged from a week-long retreat, with the words 'I've started to write a book' (that one came to nothing) just as they said to me 'You're going to write a book for our art show!'

The self-publishing of *Slippin' on the Lino* is, after some years, so much a part of who I am, that I cannot imagine a time not all that long ago when I considered myself a dabbler, rather than a writer.

I now happily call myself a writer and have since produced *In Stockmen's Footsteps* with a real publishing company, Allen & Unwin. Wearing the writer cap in public was undoubtedly one of the most difficult hurdles I overcame!

www.janegrieve.com.au

# TIME TO PRODUCE

*The process of spotting fear and refusing to obey it is the source of all true empowerment.*

~ Martha Beck

## CHAPTER 9

# FIND YOUR AUTHOR VOICE

Martha Beck, an American sociologist, life coach, best-selling author and speaker, who specialises in helping individuals and groups achieve personal and professional goals, is a big fan of dopamine. She says that creative work causes us to secrete this particular hormone, which can make us feel absorbed and fulfilled. This is in sharp contrast to the fight-or-flight mechanism, which is associated with hysteria hormones like adrenaline and cortisol.

Now, Martha is a genius, with publications such as *Finding Your North Star* and *Diana Herself* doing great work out there in the world. (In fact, her audiobook of *Finding Your Way in a Wild New World* kept me company in my car when I travelled many miles for work for a year. Londolozi, a haven in Africa where Martha hosts retreats, beckons me still.)

It's reassuring to know that even she has her bad days while putting words to page. In a recent blog post she compared herself to a dung beetle, of all things:

'*Dung beetles who can see the stars (specifically the Milky Way) roll their poo-balls in fairly straight lines. Those that can't just wander around haphazardly, probably trying to think of something interesting to write.*

*I take great comfort from this information, because I basically spend all my time rolling around a big ball of poo called My Life. I arise, make the bed, brush my teeth, and sometimes show up at my computer to work. But most of the time, like today, I don't feel I'm making any significant progress toward anything. I'm just pushing my poo-ball around, hoping no one notices that I have no idea where I'm going.*

*Today I have a gimpy back and not much pep. In five hours I've written maybe a thousand words on my current book. A few hundred of them may even be useable. Today the ball of poo feels huge, and my progress infinitesimal. It's enough to make you just stop rolling.*'

Poo-balls, indeed.

---

Challenges of writing aside (we all have our 'poo-ball' days!), the aftermath of a creative surge, especially one that involves a new skill, is a sense of accomplishment and increased self-efficacy.

I first met Viti Simmons, a leadership consultant, at a conference for regional women in leadership in Melbourne many years ago. When I offered my first online group publishing program a year or two later, I was thrilled when she signed up immediately.

Using her limited access to technology in a remote area of Western Australia, Viti joined the webinars every two weeks and made her book a priority. She has a passion for microfinance and works with not-for-profits assisting women in developing countries to change lives, so positioned her book to show what can be achieved with support. Her business is called Bear Fruit, and her first book became *A Tree Needs Water to Bear Fruit.*

During the program, Viti planned the structure of her book, and we spoke about creating deadlines, so Viti decided to launch her book at an International Women's Day function in March the following year. She had just five short months to complete writing and publishing her book, so she put her head down and did it.

She refers to that time as putting herself in her writing cave, and she accepted that she had to give up various things in order to get her book done.

On International Women's Day Viti launched her book alongside a representative from UN Women at an event in Western Australia and formed a strong connection. She has since published her second book, *Microfinance, and* her third, *Hikoi of Discovery.*

Here are some techniques Viti used to put herself in the cave. You can use them, too!

- She enabled herself to work for long stretches of time.
- She eliminated distractions. (She shut the dog outside, turned the cell phone off, etc.)
- She allowed herself breaks only at certain times.
- She was laser-focused on a deadline and had external accountability.

## CHOOSE YOUR STYLE

As you write your book, you will choose the way you present information. You decide on what style of writing personality best suits you – your author voice – and what comes most naturally to you. Here are some options:

- A pioneer – breaking new territory
- An authority – standing for what you know to be true
- An advocate – being a voice for others
- A teacher – explaining and guiding
- A mentor – modelling, encouraging, inspiring growth
- A commentator – observing and reporting
- A journalist – interviewing, researching, extrapolating and presenting
- An artist – weaving creative magic and words
- An academic – testing hypotheses, analysing, studying, digging deep
- A forecaster or oracle – presenting a wise future focus
- An inspiration – helping readers overcome odds to triumph

- A star – standing in the spotlight as the main focus
- A sage – offering trusted wisdom
- A fellow traveller – learning on the road, alongside the reader
- A satirist – exposing others' shortcomings
- A storyteller – sharing true tales
- A curator – collecting information, and sharing it in a new way

Which of these styles appeal to you? You could choose two that you are most comfortable with and use their intersection as your sweet spot – your writing voice.

Can you see how a pioneer–journalist would write in a completely different voice to an artist–sage?

## WHERE DO YOU LIKE TO WRITE?

If you're a first timer, you may have no idea. If you've never done it before, you may think that on any given day, you'll need to hole up in a dark cave, like Viti, and write for ten hours straight for fear that the ideas rattling around in your brain will be gone the next day.

Not so. Relax yourself. Choose your pace and your location. Understand your own special rhythm within your sacred, productive (and hopefully undisturbed) chunks of writing time.

Erik Larson, who famously wrote *The Devil in the White City,* has a carefully concocted list of requirements for successful writing:

- Good coffee
- More coffee
- Oreo cookies
- A fireplace (for falling asleep in front of whilst reading. After all, good writers read!)

Your list might include:

- Water views, wine and cheese
- Coffee, cake and cafés
- Ambient café sounds in your studio via www.coffitivity.com

# TIME TO WRITE

Make your book project a priority and include family and close friends in a conversation, asking them to support you and release you from other obligations at certain times, so that the book that can really impact your life, as well as theirs, is given space and freedom to grow and bloom.

When your book becomes an asset that attracts people and prosperity to you and your business in a way that matters to you, it has a ripple effect across your family too. You will then be able to support those who supported you when they helped you take time to focus on your writing. There is a positive outcome for all when you help each other achieve important goals.

Some clients set aside writing time each day; some took time out to go to a holiday location to write for a week (as I am doing right now as I type this); some negotiated a weekend away from the farm and children each month until their book was done.

Find a way that works for you, and lean into the experience of writing, rather than resisting or procrastinating. Elizabeth Gilbert says it best in *Big Magic–Creative Living Beyond Fear*:

> "Don't rush through the experiences and circumstances
> that have the most capacity to transform you.
> Don't let go of your courage the moment things stop
> being easy or rewarding. Because that moment?
> That's the moment when interesting begins."

———————

*In the next pages, or your book journal, explore the idea of being a writer, and identify your likely preferred writing style.*

# JOURNAL EXERCISE

## BECOME A WRITER

Languish over a love affair with your journal and laptop in secluded places. Grab stolen moments and develop a viewpoint where previously there may have only been an inkling.

Dream about the arty, quirky book cover which people will love and comment on. Gather photos of covers in bookstores. Create your Pinterest board.

When asked what you do, state confidently, 'I am an author,' and let yourself be carried into wonderful conversations.

**EXERCISE A:**

Which author styles would suit you and the way you think and communicate best? Refer to pages 150-151 for ideas.

**EXERCISE B:**

Spend some time here making notes about how you can arrange your activities so you have time to write. Are you a morning person? A night owl? A write-in-blocks person?

What are you willing to give up for six months to make it happen?

Sometimes the tasks you are doing as you bring a book together may not require creative ideas - sometimes you may be researching; sometimes you may be gathering content from your other assets; sometimes you may be breaking down a big idea into smaller pieces with pen and paper; sometimes you may be simply talking with others.

Don't wait for creativity to magically arrive before you begin anything ... just enjoy doing something. Anything taking you in the right direction will feel good.

# AMY ROCHE

*Author of* The Retail Experiment, *Amy is a retail and in-store customer experience engineer, and resides in Brisbane, Queensland.*

Initially, the most difficult aspect of starting the book was recognising that my own insights and learnings were valuable. With over 20 years in marketing and retail I took my own experience and specialised knowledge of running a large 2500sqm store as the norm.

I questioned what I had to say that was special or different, and why anyone would want to read my book. Despite my success in retail, it wasn't until I sat down and mapped out HOW I added $10million in turnover in two years that I saw what I had to offer. This formed the basis of my methodology, which is shared in my book, *The Retail Experiment.*

As I began to share my story verbally and socially – which was made better through my new-found clarity – I began to realise that people *really* wanted to know more about how I achieved success in retail when so many others were going backwards. I then got excited about getting my ideas out there and made time in my diary to write every day.

There is no doubt that writing the book has changed my life and my business for the better. When you're an author of a good quality book, it opens a lot more doors than you'd expect – or at least a lot more than I expected.

I never would have dreamed of receiving emails from the UAE, USA and Europe, especially since I only service Australian clients. And yes, I'm working on some new profit centres now for my overseas peeps!

I've received invitations to speak at conferences, formed national partnerships with big brands, and most of my clients now come from people who have either read my book or want to work with me because one of their colleagues has read my book.

I thought I was writing a book to boost my profile, but really it helped me with so many other things. My thought leadership is now professionally organised for me – thanks to an awesome editor. I'm constantly referring to my book to write blog posts and prepare for podcast interviews.

I think the biggest thing for me is that it has shown me through my readers' enthusiasm that my ideas aren't crazy – that they're actually helping and really resonating with my key market.

Another unexpected benefit: I used to hate public speaking, but since becoming an author I've had a lot of invitations to speak. After attending a speaker retreat with Andrew Griffiths and honing those skills, I've unexpectedly started enjoying that as well. It's also a lovely way to see more of this country and reach new retail audiences, and it has also become another income stream alongside my book sales.

www.retailrockstars.com.au

" *The best writing comes to life, and then is refined just enough to make it crystal clear. First, give it life.*

~ Audrey Owen,
author of *Writer's Helper*

## CHAPTER 10

# WRITING YOUR BOOK

Before you begin writing, take some time to go through your existing content. If you have been in business for a while and have been working with the type of people you want to address in your book, chances are you already have material in the form of blog posts, newsletters, LinkedIn articles, e-books, handouts, workbooks, tests and more. You can also transcribe audios of client conversations, webinar presentations, videos, podcast interviews and other stored material.

Your collection of gathered material, when put together, will be disjointed and fragmented, with a lot of repetition, but may provide the beginnings of your manuscript. In fact, this is how I began this book. It was a mess at that point, frankly, and has demanded much time and attention to pare it back to a useful framework, then re-shape and re-build, adding more life and texture as I progress.

**Your internal chapter structure**

Regard each chapter as a small book or stand-alone entity (or a possible e-book that you can release later as a downloadable or promotional piece) and ensure the reader understands:

4. The main point of this chapter
1. Why it is important to know this
2. The steps or information forming the main content in the chapter
3. The evidence that supports your content and proves the main point
4. Any exceptions, contradictions or obstacles that may be relevant
5. Any action the reader can take at this point.

And remember, this is a working plan – it will probably evolve as you write, but you have somewhere to begin.

**Your chapter beginnings**

Here are some ideas:

- Open the chapter with a question or two; for example, 'Have you ever allowed your fear to stop you?'
- Begin with a thought-provoking quote or statement that will immediately get the reader's attention.
- Open with an interesting fact. 'Did you know ....?'
- Begin with a short case study which shows a particular individual solving a problem.
- Quote a dramatic slice of a case study at the start of a chapter to draw the reader in, then finish the case study at the end of the chapter.

You can then tell your reader a little of what the chapter is about, and why it is important to understand this content.

**Your chapter endings**

Set aside some space at the end of each chapter to round it off and offer a reason to keep reading. Here are some ideas:

- Summary
- Questions
- Points to remember
- Action tips
- To-do list
- Checklist

* * *

When it comes down to the nitty-gritty of sentence and paragraph construction, it is difficult for anyone to tell you how to write your book. There are, however, some general writing tips to help you to DIY-edit as you progress. As you become more proficient at self-editing, you will know what to watch out for and what to avoid, and you will produce a cleaner manuscript for the editor to work on later. More on that in Chapter 12.

# WRITE WITH AUTHORITY

As you research and write about what you know, accept the fact that you can write with authority. People will listen to you because you share expertise. You are interesting because you are interested, and your passion for your topic has to shine through in your writing.

In my time as a high school English teacher it was very obvious in every school I worked in that the teachers who were loved and respected by the students were the ones who obviously loved their jobs. They might not have had a greater knowledge base than other teachers, but they were interested in the subject they taught, cared about their students, and drew the best out of them. Students loved to learn from them.

The same applies to your book. If you show passion for your subject matter, and are truly interested in your readers, draw them into your book, and show them how to achieve something important to them, you have a winning formula.

However, if you appear detached and write academically and dispassionately, you run a very real risk of losing your readers. There are millions of books in libraries which are rarely touched; I certainly don't think that's the sort of book you want to produce.

You want to write books that people interact with, write notes in, get a buzz from, recommend on social media, and pass on to friends. To write this kind of book, your interest and passion has to show – not just your interest in your topic, but also your interest in and excitement at seeing others succeed.

## LANGUAGE AND WRITING

Take the pressure off by accepting that you don't need to use impressive-sounding words with three or four syllables. Simple, down-to-earth language is fine. Use strong nouns and action verbs whenever possible.

Don't fall into the trap of thinking that your book requires corporate-speak. For example, 'utilise' is really just 'use'; 'conceptualise' really just means 'imagine'; 'volition' means 'free will'.

As for 'ideation' and 'moving the needle' … just don't.

Write an interactive book; speak directly to that one preferred reader and say to them, 'Do this, do that, think about this, act on that,' using clear language. Ask questions to give them time and space to reflect.

# ACTIVE VS. PASSIVE VOICE

Use active – as opposed to the passive – voice as much as possible in your sentences, e.g. 'The boy hit the ball' instead of 'The ball was hit by the boy'. You make a much stronger statement, and it gives your words and ideas far more authority.

'Make sure sugar is eliminated from your diet gradually' becomes 'Eliminate sugar from your diet in gradual steps'.

'Exercise needs to be a part of your life on a regular basis' becomes 'Exercise regularly'.

If you add summaries or notes and tips at the end of each chapter, begin with a command verb at the start of the sentence to entice your readers to take action.

# WRITE THE WAY YOU SPEAK

Print out a copy of your work and read it aloud. Aim to make your reader feel like they know you; that you are talking to them directly in a conversation. If your work is difficult to read aloud, or it sounds clumsy, go back and freshen it up. Give it air.

# DON'T PATRONISE YOUR READERS

Make certain that you know who you are writing for and give your audience credit for their current knowledge. Make a decision about the level of competency and understanding your readers already have on your subject and use that as a starting point. Are you writing for a layperson or beginner, rather than an intermediate or elite performer in your space?

It's critical to get that right if you want to present them with new and useful information, rather than re-hashing worn material.

## SHOW, DON'T TELL

What does it sound like, feel like, look like, smell like, taste like? If you are writing a *How-to* book, this type of language might not always apply, but you may be including features such as case studies or people's experiences, where you can add flavour and colour by 'showing' this way. Stories and characters are conveyed via actions, thoughts, words, and sensory details — instead of cold, factual exposition.

"Don't tell me the moon is shining.
Show me the glint of light on broken glass."

–Anton Chekhov

This writing technique can pull a reader into the story, so they almost feel they are experiencing it firsthand.

# VARY SENTENCE LENGTH

Vary the length of your sentences. You don't want an entire book filled with long-winded sentences: a good mix of short and long affects the overall cadence of your work. Short sentences often convey your message more clearly than longer ones, connect with the reader, and keep your writing relatable. Try it.

# COMMON STRUCTURE

It's important to keep a common structure throughout the chapters in your book and break up the text for the reader: title, sub-title, section titles throughout each chapter, breakout quotes, and other features break up large blocks of text and pull your reader in.

# VISUALS (DIAGRAMS, ILLUSTRATIONS, TABLES, GRAPHS)

If you're struggling to find a way to get a particular message across, perhaps a simple visual representation will work best. People process information in different ways, so find ways to add these elements if you feel they work for your audience. Your graphic designer will take your amateurish sketches and make them look smart when your pages are done.

# STORIES AND CASE STUDIES

In *The Story Factor*, Annette Simmons extols the value of stories in presentations: adding stories or case studies to exemplify key points or inspire others to achieve will draw your audience around you and engage with them directly.

The author Lisa Cron has written three books on storytelling, and her most recent one, *Story or Die*, is probably most relevant to non-fiction authors who are writing books to enhance their business and brand. Memoir writers will find all three useful:

- *Wired for Story: The Writer's Guide to Using Brain Science to Hook Readers from the Very First Sentence* (2012)
- *Story Genius: How to Use Brain Science to Go Beyond Outlining and Write a Riveting Novel (2016)*
- *Story or Die: How to Use Brain Science to Engage, Persuade, and Change Minds in Business and in Life (2021)*

# OTHER ADDITIONS OF VALUE

Quotes – people love them. Keep them relevant. Use other people's quotes or use your own words from the text and feature those.

Consider adding a recommended reading list or list of resources to your book for added value.

If you'd like to include worksheets in your book, consider producing two versions—your standard sized business book and a separate larger workbook. You can sell these separately or package them together and charge accordingly, or provide them at workshops, etc.

# PRESENTING INFORMATION

Here are some useful ways of presenting information, as covered fully in the highly commended 'Think on Your Feet®' communication program. You could use these structures within case studies, sections, whole chapters or even your book itself.

### Time order

The simplest way to format information is to move through time. The format is clear and easy to understand because it is simply a matter of past-present-future. However, it should be mentioned that you don't necessarily have to follow that order.

### Location

If you are writing about a topic that is global in nature yet varies from country to country, a geographical structure could be very useful. For example, you could compare organic food production across various countries, or resource management, or parenting practices. You can also talk about geographical locations on a smaller scale; for example, best practice in various locations within a business: the factory floor, in the office and on the client's site, and more.

## Three views

This is a useful way to objectively present a number of viewpoints on a subject. An example: a book containing the latest education theory for at-risk adolescents could contain the viewpoints of a teen, an educational development expert, and a psychologist. Presenting a 'triangle' of views is an excellent way of keeping your book relevant and interesting for the reader.

## Focus in and out

You can use the focus technique for the overall structure of your book, or only in those sections where it would be a particularly useful way to highlight the general and the specific of an issue you're discussing. You might zoom in by writing a story or analysis of that specific issue, and when zooming out, you present a larger, wider view.

## Opposites

You might use this technique to present extreme viewpoints on an issue or topic – one on the left and one on the right – before moving to the safer middle ground. It is a very persuasive technique, particularly if your intention is to get people to accept or choose that middle option after understanding the extremes.

## Advantages

This technique is useful early in a book if you want to structure your content as providing benefits. A sound strategy is to place the weakest benefit in the middle, while opening and closing with the stronger benefits.

# WRITING BOOK TITLES, SUB-TITLES & CHAPTER TITLES

Non-fiction book titles and sub-titles must tell your preferred reader what the book is about and offer a major benefit in exchange for their time. Usually the sub-title does the heavy lifting or convincing.

The book *Write It Down, Make It Happen* offers an excellent example of command language, with a sub-title of *Knowing What You Want–And Getting It*, offering a high-level benefit.

Here are some examples of clients' books:

- *Accreditation Ready: Smart Strategies for Successful Stress-Free Audits* by Felicity Hamilton
- *Your Future–Shape It: 6 Steps to Financial Peace of Mind* by Geoff Orr
- *Women as Leaders: The World Needs You* by Denise Gibbons
- *High Thrive Me! A 5-step guide to helping kids with autism live happier, healthier lives* by Kris Barrett

## CHAPTER TITLES

Regard each chapter title as a mini-book title. The chapter titles need to pull the reader in, so apply the same rules to chapter titles that you do to your book title. Chapter titles can become keywords in all sorts of contexts in internet searches. If at some point you split your book up into individual little e-books, then your chapter title actually becomes a book title.

**TIP:** Use online keyword research tools such as Keyword Tool (www.keywordtool.io) to find what your target audience is searching for most frequently that is directly relevant to your book. Look at how you might include those words in your book's titles and content, as well as your website and other online presences you have.

# TITLE IDEAS

Here are some tried and tested title formats of real books, which could inspire you with your book title, sub-title or chapter titles:

- *Nine Steps to Success*
- *7 Steps to Health*
- *The 7 Habits of Highly Effective People*
- *The Insider's Guide to Building a Successful Consulting Practice*
- *The Insider's Guide to the Oregon Coast*
- *Top Secret Restaurant Recipes*
- *Nine Secrets of the Rich and Famous*
- *The Expert's Guide to Weight-Loss Surgery*
- *The Expert's Guide to Collecting & Investing in Rare Coins*
- *The Truth About Cancer*
- *Seven Myths about Education*
- *The E-Myth*
- *How to Win Friends & Influence People*
- *How to Draw Cool Stuff*
- *Become a Key Person of Influence*
- *Think & Grow Rich*
- *Think, Learn, Succeed*

And more recently, the short and sharp title is a winner – always accompanied by informative sub-titles:

- *Lean In; Play Big; Dare to Lead; Amplify; Altitude; Elevate*

# JOURNAL EXERCISE

## TITLES

Write down the key benefits your reader will get from reading your book.

Can you create your ideal sub-title from that list?

Play about with some book title ideas. The title is usually short and sharp, and suggests a win or positive outcome. Don't use negative words.

The sub-title is a longer piece that expands on the title and shows the benefits of taking action, based on what the reader will learn from your book.

Use the ideas in Chapter 10 to inspire you. Research other books in your type in Amazon to see how other writers do this. Some will be better than others.

Research top-selling books for ideas, language patterns, and promises to the reader implicit in their titles and sub-titles.

# DOLORES CUMMINS

*Co-author of* Altitude–Two Women's Journey on Mt Kilimanjaro, *with Barbara Baikie, Dolores is an executive coach, business leader and world traveller, currently in Sydney, Australia.*

One of the most difficult aspects of co-writing the book was valuing my own voice. Initially this book started as a leadership book backed up by other people's voices and lots of theory. It was dry and flat. When I finally dared to add my own voice and story, it became real. By believing I had something worthwhile to contribute, I gave myself permission to be visible. The vulnerability was palpable.

The most difficult aspect of the publishing process was not knowing how or where to start. A chance encounter with Bev Ryan at a women's business event proved to be the catalyst that forged a new pathway.

While there were still many challenges along the way, like remaining disciplined about regular writing, and dealing with the daunting task of re-structuring the book during editing, having a structured step-by-step plan helped.

Writing and publishing *Altitude* has opened up many opportunities for new coaching and consulting work, speaking engagements, and introductions to key influencers. It has also allowed me to not just become a newly visible voice but also to stand more confidently in that voice.

The greatest rewards to me are being acknowledged by others and coming to my own understanding about just what is possible when you set your mind to it.

Publishing a book really does give you credibility to a wide scope of diverse people and communities.

www.dolorescummins.com

*Opportunity is missed by most people because it is dressed in overalls and looks like work.*

~ Thomas Edison

## CHAPTER 11

# FUNDING IDEAS

I advocate self-publishing as the perfect path when becoming a business author, because you are already a decision maker; you understand product and service development; you get the importance of sales and marketing; you have valuable intellectual property (probably more than you realise); and you know how to make things happen.

Pitching a book idea to an agent and then to a publishing company seems to me like standing in a queue with your hands out, begging for a crumb. You don't need to do that!

We are so fortunate to have access to the technology and skills we need, anywhere in the world, to unleash our creative and enterprising selves and publish – whether that be music, artwork, songs, films, books, games and so much more.

Show your initiative, determination and spirit. Back your dream and make it happen.

Here are some ways to raise some necessary capital, if that is a consideration for you. (I cover estimated costs in Chapter 12.)

## PRE-SALES

Your book cover image and back cover sales blurb can be used for promotional purposes well before the book is ready to sell, so it is important to get that done as early as possible, while you are still in the writing process. Add that information to your website when your book goal is in sight. If you speak at a conference before your book is ready, do a promotion and offer a special pre-order price, capturing buyers' details and pre-payment – or at least the email addresses of interested people.

## SPONSORSHIPS

In the (diminishing) magazine publishing world, advertising has always been a critical part of the money equation. A well-orchestrated magazine gathers a particular audience around a niched subject matter with interesting content – think cars, boats, running, luxury homes, weddings, home renovation, alternative living and so much more – and advertisers pay to pop their head up and say hello to the readership.

Of course, the price advertisers pay depends on the number of readers they can be almost guaranteed to reach. The onus on converting that reach to sales lies with the company running the ads, rather than the publisher.

Although the magazine industry has been shaken up by digital publishing, it still offers some concepts that you can perhaps apply to your book.

Call it sponsorship if you prefer. Are there companies who would love to align with you and/or reach your intended readership, and would see benefit from appearing in your pages? Is there room for a partnership where you promote them to your new readers, and they promote your book to their existing followers?

I have paid for a half-page promotion within a business book published by a well-known business coach who uses publishing as one of her key business growth strategies. (On reflection, I would now choose the full-page option, so my message is not lost in the noise.)

Several book clients have received help to pay for their book production costs by selling full-page and half-page advertising spaces at the front or back of their specifically niched books.

Can you offer a bundle to sponsors? Here are some ideas:

Advertising space on your cover or in your book (on a page in the front, middle or back)

Their content on one side of your bookmark

Their postcard or sheet inserted into every book as it is printed or packaged

Their content on your website and in your newsletter

A display and presentation presence at your online or in-person events?

## CO-BRANDING AND PARTNERSHIPS

There is no limit to the creative ways businesses can work together for a common good and find inspiring ways to provide value to a common audience.

Some authors just create valued content and licence others to publish and sell their material for a fee and ongoing royalties. Think Kate Knapp, Australian author and artist, and creator of Twigseeds, whose art now adorns products sold internationally: www. twigseeds.com

Some authors sell branding rights to companies, which allow the company to add their logo and/or other visual elements to the book cover and within the book, then print a special run or runs of the book for distribution to their own client base.

# CROWD FUNDING LITERARY AGENCY: PUBLISHIZER

Publishizer is a book crowdfunding platform and literary agency that matches authors with publishers. This service began the way of every startup, with a big idea and a small amount of money, and is now humming along, showing some heart-warming author success stories on their homepage.

The site services authors seeking funding through pre-sales of their book, or their book plus other bundled services such as coaching, workshops, speaking, and consulting. During your campaign, you attract interest to your Publishizer page and buyers can pre-order one or more of your variously priced offers while the book is being written.

Basically you can pre-sell your book, as well as other business offers, ranging in price from $20 to thousands of dollars. Brilliant!

The site now also facilitates a literary agency of sorts, where publishing companies can approach authors they are interested in and offer publishing services or publishing contracts, or that hybrid mix we spoke about earlier.

**How It Works**

No book manuscript is required. Use their Publishizer book proposal template (like the book plan described here in Chapter 6) and submit a professional book proposal that meets industry standards.

For 30 days, publishers receive a weekly round-up that includes your proposal.

You disseminate and promote your funding page on Publishizer every which-way that you can, and pre-sell copies of your book and bundled offers. If that performs well, you may attract a direct pitch to the inboxes of traditional advance-paying publishers.

Publishers express interest in your book via the site, and you can respond to the publishers you're interested in. The site offers support and guidance from registration right through to signing a publishing deal.

The site receives a percentage of funds raised as their fee. See more at www.publishizer.com.

# JOURNAL EXERCISE

## FUNDING

Put your thinking cap on: can you see any win-win situations you could initiate? This is where your Book Business Plan comes to the fore. Much of that content can be moulded into convincing sponsorship or partnership proposals.

The best place to start is by talking to people you know – or placing a call-out in online groups or networks you belong to. LinkedIn is an excellent place to find people in the right places. (Make sure your own profile reflects the professionalism you desire to attract.)

This added activity may slow down your progress with your book – or the funding may allow you to submerge yourself in it totally and get it done sooner that you had thought.

Write down some free-flowing ideas about funding your book here.

# BETH JENNINGS

*Beth is an Australian photographer and author of* Memories at Your Fingertips *and* She knows. *She crowdfunded her first book.*

The process of writing my first book about digital photos, *Memories at Your Fingertips* was, for the most part, pretty seamless. The book added immeasurable credibility to my profile and acts as a wonderful gift to clients when we come to the end of our working relationship. It contains so many topics to draw on for public speaking and media, both of which have happened to me since the book. So it has brought attention to my business that was not there before.

This attention was also self-generated when I successfully raised $11,305 via a crowdfunding campaign. The essence of the campaign was to pre-sell the book, and in doing so, fund it's editing, design and first 100 print copies. This exercise also allowed me to test the book concept in the market before it had actually gone to production. Given its positive acceptance and support, I was able to proceed with confidence that the book had potential and relevance.

I didn't expect how publishing the first book would make me see myself. There is nothing more concrete than a book to prove that 'you know your stuff'. It makes an indelible impression on others, but also on me too in terms of my confidence. It drives these other activities (such as media and public speaking) which in turn deliver a raise in confidence.

When I began writing my second book, I parked my reservations and followed a proposed formula that works for others. I created a skeleton book of 15,000 words that addressed my clients' three main problems and then solved those with the why, what, how structure. Awesome!

But that book didn't feel right. It felt tight and I felt bored with it: it was neither stimulating nor exciting. When I thought about holding this book and presenting it to people, I could feel a cringe.

I later realised, 'I don't see why I can't write an inspirational book, which IS my business book. I've seen plenty of other photographers showcase their work in an inspirational way and it positions them as specialised in their preferred field. Why can't I do that?'

I loved the idea of writing a book that was centred around inspirational stories and photographs of women, more so than problem solving. The artist in me felt excited, and so *She knows* was born. As I went along through the creative process and unravelled some of the issues, it then became important for this book to express something unique about me, my vulnerabilities and honesty.

There is something powerful and hard to explain about the physical manifestation of what was in my head and heart into this thing I can actually hold in my hands and give to people. I can't emphasise enough the feeling of power it gives me in its physical form. I didn't expect that to be as intense as it is.

www.bethjenningsphotography.com

# TIME TO PUBLISH
# AND MARKET

*Perfectionism is the voice of the oppressor, the enemy of the people. It will keep you cramped and insane your whole life, and it is the main obstacle between you and a shitty first draft.*

~ Anne Lamott in *Bird by Bird: Some Instructions on Writing and Life*

## CHAPTER 12

# THE BOOK CREATION STAGE

Perfectionism masquerading as procrastination – or is the other way round? – often traps emerging authors in the unchartered space between their own 'shitty first draft' hiding on their PC, and the quite exposed and vulnerable construction site for this new and beautiful thing called their book.

At some stage your collection of words – some genius, some scruffy – must pass through the ether into the hands of the experts who will then chip away quietly, trimming, shaping, polishing, dreaming and designing, until this tangible, creative thing appears in a box one day at your door.

Pretty exciting stuff!

In this chapter you will learn more about these creative steps involved after you push 'send' on the email containing your manuscript to your editor:

Cover design
Editing
Page design and layout
Proofreading
Printing
Online distribution
Bookstore distribution

## COVER DESIGN

Work with a good designer while you are writing your book, or during the editing phase at the very latest.

Firstly, the process will force you to make some critical decisions about your book, like size, title and sub-title, book description, and author bio.

Secondly, you can use the cover image to begin raising awareness of your book. Place an image of your front cover on your website, with the facility for others to express interest in its arrival, or even pre-purchase. Use it in your email signature with the phrase, 'Author of the forthcoming book,' so even before you finish writing, you have created some leverage.

Begin thinking about your book cover design and book title now by browsing in bookstores (and taking sneaky photos), looking at online bookstores, searching on Pinterest, googling 'best book covers ever', looking at publishing companies' websites and more. Create your own folder or Pinterest board and build a collection.

The other essential part of a good book cover is the back cover sales copy. It should say to the potential buyer, 'You need me!', so you might like to hire a copywriter to assist with that, as well as other marketing material like your book's webpage, and even your author bio.

Allow about four weeks to work with a designer on your cover.

**DOWNLOAD** a checklist of features that appear in a good book cover design at www.smartwomenpublish.com/extras.

# EDITING

There's no question about it, you need an editor because they will provide the objective feedback your book needs so that it becomes the best it can possibly be.

Before you send everything off to them though, review your manuscript again after at least a week's break from it. You will see it with fresh eyes and pick up changes you can easily make yourself.

Once the editing is underway, the process can take a month or more, depending on the complexity and length of the manuscript. The amount an editor charges is based on what your book needs at any particular stage. The major types of editing include:

- Full edit (sometimes called substantive, comprehensive, or developmental editing): This involves heavy work and detailed editing to the overall book structure.
- Copy edit/line edit: This type of editing drills into your book by looking closely at every line to be sure each sentence flows smoothly, and the content is cohesive.
- Proofreading: This is not an edit. It is a check and fix of grammar, punctuation, spelling, layout and more.

You're still the author and you steer the ship. If you have a good editor, he or she will be your guide and won't commandeer the entire project. It should be a partnership that has one goal: to make your book the absolute best it can be.

---

# PAGE DESIGN AND LAYOUT

When the editor is finished, it is time to move on to the layout of your book, where the graphic designer of your choice turns your manuscript into a professionally finished product that will look at home in a quality bookstore.

Several page design options are created around the cover design, so it is important to do the cover first. Once you finalise the page design of your choice, which may involve some design tweaking and adjustments on a sample chapter, the full page layout begins. The first layout can happen quite quickly – a matter of days – but it is critical that there is then time for thoughtful review, further proofreading, and the inevitable changes – which then must be proofed again. Three weeks is a good time frame for this.

# PURCHASE YOUR ISBN & BARCODE

Go to myidentifiers.com.au where you can purchase your ISBN on the spot. Be careful though: the site gives you the option to buy one for $44 or a set of ten for $88 (subject to change). I advise the latter because you can then assign unique numbers to your print book and e-book versions – as well as future books. You also purchase barcodes for print books on this site.

# PROOFREADING

Once the book pages are fully designed, allow another week or two for a professional and thorough proofread. It is critical that a trained eye does this because they know what errors and layout glitches to look out for. The designer then makes adjustments, which must be checked again, and so it continues. You must also do a final proofread at this stage because as a self-publisher, you take full responsibility for the final product.

# FILE PREPARATION

Eventually it is time to finalise your book cover and page layout and store the files in one location. They remain separate files, and each one must be saved properly in the formats required by your printer; Amazon Kindle; your online print-on-demand company of choice; and Apple Books. Your designer knows what to do. If they don't, they should not be working on your book.

# PRINTING

You no longer have to source money for high up-front costs of large print-runs of your book, if you do not want to go that way. Small manageable print runs and ongoing online print-on-demand are now worthy options.

Many self-publishers organise a print run of books from a print business when their files are ready to go. Companies specialising in print books now use large heavy-duty digital book printers and binders, and deliver a stock of high quality books to your door in weeks. A very exciting day in the life of an author!

You also have the option of arranging less costly print services offshore, and it is best to do that through a reputable print broker in Australia. This will add up to eight weeks to your schedule.

This is also the appropriate time to mention print on demand (POD) with IngramSpark, which also provides print and e-book distribution. You can set up an account online and take control of your own publishing business when your print and e-book files are lodged with them. They have print facilities all over the world, with a network of warehouses, retailers, libraries, distributors, and readers. Your print book goes into their catalogue, which book retailers access and order from. Your book also appears on Amazon and other sites, where customers can purchase it. IngramSpark receives the order, prints a copy, and ships it to them.

You can also log in to your account and order stock for yourself at wholesale prices. See more at www.ingramspark.com.

## ONLINE DISTRIBUTION

E-books are more of a level playing field between self-publishers and commercial operators. They can be distributed online via your own site or using a distribution channel such as Amazon Kindle or IngramSpark for iTunes/iBooks. There will be various terms and conditions associated with using a third party distribution service. For example, the royalty rates on books distributed by Amazon vary depending on the price that is charged. This will obviously affect your financial return compared to distributing your e-book online via your own channel, but on the plus side, you won't have the need to set up e-commerce facilities on your own site.

The most common e-book formats are .epub, .mobi and pdf, which your book designer will supply after the book is fully designed.

## BOOKSTORES

Book distribution companies deliver books to bookstores and self-publishers can certainly approach them on their own behalf. Distribution companies base their decision to handle self-published authors' books on sales potential; professional presentation of your book; and the author's own profile and potential to push sales. The company profits from a share in your sales, as does the bookstore. Distributors do not market your book – that is up to you – although they do assist with creating marketing material for use in the stores if you invest in that added extra.

Print book distribution companies may also require sole rights sell your print books in Australia.

The obvious question to ask yourself is this: Are my ideal readers more likely to wander into a bookstore looking for a book like mine, or are they more likely to search for a book like mine online and quickly and easily purchase a print-on-demand copy?

This is not an endorsement for the following distribution companies as I have no personal experience with these companies as I write this, but some options are:

1. Woodslane (www.woodslane.com.au)
2. John Reed Books may distribute books for individual members of the Australian Society of Authors (begin at www.asauthors.org)

Booktopia Publishing Services (BPS) is a full-service book distributor, providing a unique solution for publishers (not individual authors) wanting to maximise their exposure in the Australia and New Zealand market.

You can also approach bookstores yourself, armed with a copy of your book and your book business plan to show them how they might profit from your product as well.

## COST OF SERVICES

As you will appreciate, every book requires its own level of attention.

Manuscript drafts vary in length. Some are poorly written and require a lot of remedial attention during editing; others are well-constructed and an editor's dream.

Book covers sometimes come together easily, especially when the author and designer have a similar concept in mind. Sometimes they take time because of the level of design construction required, or the author swings between many design ideas and becomes indecisive and afraid of commitment. The more hours it takes, the more it will cost.

Page layouts are sometimes straight-forward; other times the designer may have to construct imagery and tables; juggle lengthy complex content; add colour elements; or deal with that indecisive client again.

Again, the cost is determined by the time it takes.

Printers require full specifications for a book before they will quote a cost. Ask your editor or designer to estimate the number of pages in your book and decide on your book dimensions before contacting printers for comparative quotes.

## Estimates

Here are some estimates for a 35,000 word business book, with colour cover, black and white pages, and a few diagrams and tables. These are just estimates, keep in mind, as prices differ from one supplier to another, and every book is unique.

As a self-publisher you can chase all of these quotes and costs individually – and trust that you find good people – or you might consider the option of a one-stop publishing service. (See final page of this book.) They charge one fee and include all services as well as a project manager who is your one point of contact and who coordinates and quality controls everything for you. You retain full ownership of all files and all proceeds of sales – it is not an ongoing relationship with ongoing fees.

- Review: $1000–$2000 (feedback on book under construction – optional)
- Full edit: $2000–$3500
- Manuscript proofread only: $1000–$2000
- Book cover design: $500–$2000
- Page layout: $800–$2000 (more for full-colour visual treats)
- Pre-print proofread: $800–$1500
- Printing: 200 copies – unit price between $5 and $10 (more for full colour and/or hardcover)

---

*During the following exercise think about the cost of publishing, as well as the benefits of investing in a book as a leap forward.*

# JOURNAL EXERCISE

## INVESTMENT

Calculate a rough estimate of the cost of self-publishing your book.

Keep in mind that you are creating a product for your business – and educating yourself – as well as elevating your visibility and amplifying your voice. It is a marketing and branding project that will bring a return on investment for years, as well as an education program, and product development process.

What is that worth to you?

If not with a book, how would you do that otherwise?

How will you fund your book production when you get to that point – keeping in mind that it costs nothing to begin writing now? You don't need to know how: you just need to believe you will, and seek the help you need. A book coach is the perfect person to ensure you get your book well underway, with professional guidance.

# BRONWYN REID

---

*Author of* Small Company, Big Business - how to get your small business ready to do business with big business, *Bronwyn is a business consultant, mentor and educator, based in Central Queensland.*

My book is for small to medium business owners who have built a successful business, but now want to step up their company growth by taking on contracts with a large organisation. This can be extremely valuable, but it's not easy. Big organisations set a high bar for their suppliers and expect those high standards to be maintained. My book describes the five steps that a small business owner must take in order to become a capable, reliable and profitable supplier to their potential big customers.

I started writing my book at a very turbulent time in our business. Finding time and headspace was extremely difficult. It took me longer than it should have to get this book finished because of imposter syndrome, but a severe talking-to from one of my mentors was the catalyst for me to finally get it finished.

Being a published author certainly gives an additional boost to my profile. My book grew out of my many years of experience in our existing business, and having it completed has allowed me to launch a new business in an entirely new direction. I am now being invited to deliver speaking engagements and workshops. I have been consulted by the Australian Government and other

---

semi-government authorities, and in late 2018 I presented for the first time at an international conference.

Interestingly, I am now being drawn into yet another related business topic as well, as a result of speaking engagements around the book. So, once the book is released to the world, you never quite know where it will take you.

www.bronwynreid.com.au

*You have to believe, in the deepest part of your soul, that it is a good thing for readers to buy and read your book.*

~ Tim Grahl,
author of *Book Launch Blueprint*

CHAPTER 13

# PREPARE FOR LAUNCH AND LEVERAGE

A s a business owner who is planning to write a book, you will already understand how important a growing database of preferred clients is to your ongoing success. Hopefully you have that under control. And if you are writing your book to ultimately share your expertise, build your profile and grow your business, many of your ideal readers are already on your list. However, the more you can build up your network of followers and connections via social media, and find ways to move them onto your mailing list, the better off you are going to be when the time comes to market your book.

You will hear much about author platforms: this is simply a marketing term that means all of the ways you are going to connect with people and sell your book. Yours will be a growing mix of the following:

- your existing and new business clients
- increasing opportunities to speak at small and large events
- followers of your blog and/or newsletter subscribers
- Facebook, Twitter, LinkedIn, Pinterest and Instagram followers, etc.
- online groups you manage or co-manage, e.g. LinkedIn, Meetup, Facebook
- social or business gatherings you attend
- exclusive VIP group events you run or co-host
- podcast and YouTube followers
- memberships of networks and professional organisations
- mutually beneficial relationships with others with leverage
- your increasing profile in mainstream media (radio, TV, newspapers, magazines, etc.)

Become active on the social media outlets which appeal and attract your target readership. If you are writing a cookbook with lovely visuals, Pinterest, Facebook and Instagram might work best for you. If you are writing a book for business, LinkedIn is ideal. On Facebook, find groups that revolve around your book message.

# PRE-PUBLISHING ACTIVITY

## Website

Developing a specific website for your book prior to its publication and potentially having a launch event are other promotional methods you can use. Make sure you hire a web designer to build your website though, so that it doesn't look too amateurish. Your promotional efforts should look professional, reflect the quality of your book (which you will ensure is bookstore-worthy as a benchmark), and the quality of the clients you wish to attract.

You can also maximise the search engine optimisation of your website. This can be done by using keywords on your site that match those used by your target market when doing Google searches for book-related topics.

In addition, targeted and cost-effective online advertising via social media is an option to consider, as well as advertising on other online sites relevant to the topic of your book. These options will all provide additional exposure to your target market.

## Test marketing

Ideally, you should think about marketing your book as soon as you start developing your topic and content ideas, as well as throughout the writing process. This will allow you to do some test marketing along the way. For example, you can include a test marketing webpage on your website or on your social media sites prior to publication. This can help you get invaluable feedback that you can use to make your book more marketable when it actually comes time to launch it. Hopefully it will also provide you with positive energy and motivation to keep going.

You don't necessarily need to make a test marketing page for your book available to the general public. Instead, set restrictions so only selected people have access. This lets key people in your network know about your book and builds anticipation (and hopefully future sales)!

You can obtain feedback by sharing the page link and ensuring there is a facility for people to leave their comments and suggestions. For example, you can put your ideas for the front and back cover designs on there, and let people vote for the one they like best. You could also include some brief information about the book, including the benefits of reading it. If there is any other information you want for your book, consider having a short survey for people to fill out.

You could also add a PayPal button and offer a pre-launch discount for people who help you with your test marketing research. For example, if your book will be priced at $29, you could offer participants in your test marketing exercise a special pre-launch sale price of $15 or $20. However, if you take this pre-purchase approach and start accepting money, you'll need to make it very clear when the book will be available for those purchasers. Your publishing plan and timelines will need to be firm.

**Reviews and testimonials**

Getting favourable reviews and testimonials from readers can be another effective way of promoting your book once it is published.

These can be particularly impactful if the reviewer is credible and therefore likely to be an influencer on social media platforms. Reviews and testimonials can even be obtained prior to publication by negotiating with key people and providing them with a copy of your manuscript. Favourable comments could be included on the back cover blurb, in the front of the book itself (as I have done in this book), as well as online in promotional material.

## Pre-promotions

Remember in Chapter 3 I asked you to work on your author self-image? Here are a few ideas that will help you put this into practice in your world. (If you catch yourself pulling back, listen to what your paradigms are telling you. That's where you need to do some work.)

As you write your book, begin telling the world about it in various ways:

- ☐ Add your version of this statement – 'Author of the forthcoming book, *Write Winning Proposals*' – to your email signature, your LinkedIn profile, your website, your Facebook page, and anywhere else you can.
- ☐ Add that phrase plus your book's sub-title to all printed introductions, your speaker bio, media kit, and more.
- ☐ Include your coming book title whenever you introduce yourself in a business context, whether requesting a first meeting, pitching for business or partnerships, or at business events.

- ☐ Add your book information when applying for awards, speaking segments at conferences, podcast guest spots, or guest blogging gigs.
- ☐ Plan a schedule of events that you will be holding and promote the event and yourself as host using the information about your coming book.

All of these simple methods can have a measurable impact on your client numbers, quality of clients, the fees you can charge, speaking invitations, media opportunities, sales conversions, and more.

You will also be delighted by the interest people show in your book and your author journey. Open up to conversations and share what you are doing, even though you may feel a little shy about it, as you never know where they will eventually lead.

## BOOK MARKETING MATERIAL

Prepare your book marketing material before your book is launched and use it in the lead-up.

Think movie trailer without the over-dramatic music and voice-over. Create a few short videos that connect with your target audience and highlight the promise your book makes to them, then provide an online home where people can easily go to connect with you or register their interest with the click of a mouse or a few strokes on the keyboard.

Use your front cover design, or elements of it, as the basis for postcards, bookmarks, thank-you notes, your business card, posters, flyers, speaker and media kits, website and social media banners, social media imagery and more.

For events, use a pull-up banner which is designed well and includes you and your book. You can also purchase backdrops for your office use when sitting at your desk speaking on camera with clients or in groups. The alternative is a green screen background and a branded image that you use as your virtual backdrop during webinars with systems such as Zoom.

## CONTENT MARKETING

Be the expert – provide content showing others how to have more, do more and be more.

Online marketing is cheaper and can often be more targeted and effective than traditional marketing efforts such as personal selling or print advertising. During the writing process, you can develop contacts in your target market via social media platforms such as Facebook, Twitter and LinkedIn. This can help you to build an online database of potential readers to target more intensively when your book is published. You can also develop your personal online brand and profile by commenting in relevant forums, writing online articles or physically attending events to network with like-minded people.

What videos, webinars, social media updates, newsletters and articles can you create around the key issues you care about and that your book addresses?

As you write your book you are already knee-deep in material. If you cull something because it is not quite right, save it for another use. Right now I have a Google doc named 'Spare material' containing cuts from this book, for that exact purpose. It will be easy to find sentences, paragraphs and ideas for simple social media or quick blog posts every now and then.

Here are some ideas, but ultimately, it's up to you to use your creativity to unleash your own brand onto the world.

**Bonus material:** Create an independent addendum to your book that can be just for your readers: an extra chapter, a vlog, a special guide, mini-book, etc. to add to what readers will or have already gotten from your book. Don't forget to have readers opt in to your email list in order to receive whatever you've decided will be your bonus material.

**Webinars/regular classes:** They are all a great way to add value to your book and your brand by teaching what you know. Many of your students will have already read your book and will be looking for you to add more value to what they've read.

**Coaching or consulting:** Much like teaching, coaching and consulting are powerful ways to add to your brand and offer a high level of value.

**VIP days:** Develop high-end intense one-day or two-day coaching or mentoring options, delivered exclusively to individuals or very small, exclusive groups, where entry is via application only.

**Free online groups:** Set up a closed Facebook group for your book and invite people to join you there for a more relaxed and ongoing connection with you, where you provide encouragement and information relevant to your expertise, or simply answer questions in your area of expertise.

# BOOK LAUNCHES

Don't feel you have to create one big, expensive live event for a book launch. It's your book and your business, so promote and celebrate your book in ongoing ways (yes, plural) that honour your readers and reflect your business and style.

Firstly, celebrate over a meal with family and friends. It's a big deal.

Then I suggest you plan several book launch events for different purposes and audiences. Here are just some opportunities to bring people together and gain some valuable visibility and traction for your business:

### Host a VIP dinner

Invite a select group of influential and well-connected people to a classy dinner, which you might pay for. Facilitate some valuable networking within the room, talk a little about the book and what you hope to achieve with it in business terms, and open the floor up to some informal brainstorming. You will be amazed by what transpires then and later.

### Run an event

Invite large numbers to a breakfast, lunch or dinner where you deliver a valuable presentation based on the content in your book. Guests pay to attend, learn something of value to them, and receive your book as part of the package.

### Launch at a larger industry event

Viti Simmons, author of *A Tree Needs Water to Bear Fruit*, launched her book about alleviation of poverty at a UN Women event in Western Australia on International Women's Day.

Christine Franklin, author of *The Extra Mile*, launched her book supporting rural health practitioners at a national conference on rural and regional health.

Look out for forthcoming events where your ideal readership will be represented, and people of influence will be attending as speakers and presenters. Take the initiative and contact the organisers, and find a win-win situation where all will benefit from you launching your book there.

### Create an online launch

Find out more about virtual book launches by searching that term on Facebook, and joining or observing the many launch events that occur there. They may take place for an hour, a day, a week or a month. You set up the launch event and orchestrate the promotional activities, presentations and follow-up. Engage as many social media channels as you wish in the promotional process and follow-up; invite guests to join you and ask them to promote the event to their audience; prepare all materials you need in the promotional stage, such as digital book trailer, visuals, short video clips and more, all pointing people back to the launch event.

## CREATE A VIRTUAL BOOK INTERVIEW TOUR

With the rapid growth in podcasts you will find hosts all over the world regularly broadcasting content to people who are your ideal readers, so approach them about being a guest and offer content that helps their listeners in some way. Promote their podcasts to your audiences as well and it becomes a win-win. Map out a regular string of speaking engagements that will probably flow on to more invitations and opportunities.

## GIVE YOUR BOOK AWAY

When you are publishing a book to grow your business, rather than just profit from book sales, you will see the logic in applying this generous strategy from time to time. After all, which would you prefer – working hard to achieve a low number of sales, or high visibility and good energy as your book circulates?

When you receive your first batch of books from the printer, be ready to post attractively wrapped copies, with hand-written notes, to people of influence – people you may already know and people you have not yet met.

Gift your book to potential clients, at events, and during conversations where you discover a common link. Books that authors have shared with a fellow passenger during plane flights have later led to unexpected invitations to speak, consult, mentor and more.

You can also promote an offer to give your print book away to people for a period of time, and ask them to just cover postage. In return, you are building a database of contacts who are interested in your material, know who you are, and who may then be interested in another easily affordable service or product you offer later.

Seth Godin, now a renowned author, self-published *Purple Cow* after being rejected by publishers. He printed 10,000 copies and gifted them for the cost of the postage. Not long after, a publishing company bought the rights to the book and sold 250,000 copies later that year.

Jeff Goins, writer, convinced the publisher of his first trade book to give away hundreds of copies when it was launched (something they don't like to do), and it went on to sell 20,000 copies in the first six months because it was out and about, and visible.

Apply this same principle to gifting a pdf version of your book online for a period of time, in order to build your email list of interested, pre-qualified people. You can then follow up with promotions of events, services and other offers. Callan Rush does this brilliantly with her free downloadable book, *Wealth Through Workshops*, which is the easy entry point to her very successful international training and coaching business.

———————

*In the next exercise, spend time focusing on how you will contribute to others and build connections.*

# JOURNAL EXERCISE

## YOUR CONNECTIONS

*Marketing is the art of building long-lasting connections and being relentlessly helpful*

~ Tim Grahl, author of *Your First 1000 Copies*

Make notes here or in your journal about the current state of your 'author platform':

- your email list and how often they hear from you
- online networks and groups
- in-person networks and groups
- LinkedIn connections
- Facebook connections
- Instagram connections
- Other

How can you increase your activity a little (if you have been quiet)? How can you begin to gather more subscribers and followers by being relentlessly helpful – in a way that is connected to the book you would love to write?

Where online would you find potential readers for your book? Which of those platforms do you enjoy the most? Begin there, focus, and become more helpful and visible.

# ANNE GALLOWAY

*Anne and Ian Galloway are highly respected Queensland beef producers who commissioned five freelance writers to profile 28 successful and enterprising women in the cattle industry in the book Cattlemen in Pearls – Celebrating Women in Agriculture.*

Due to established industry partnerships, sales of this high-quality full-colour book have been very successful since its launch in August 2018, selling out the first print run of 1500 books within three months via the book's website, in stores and at events. Second and third print runs were completed, and more than 4000 books sold before the year's end.

The book was launched by Pip Courtney from ABC Landline to a large gathering at a women's high tea at the Royal Queensland Show, and 400 copies were sold at that first event. Pip graciously wrote a testimonial for the back cover and has featured the book in an ABC Landline episode as well.

Post-launch our book stockists have been regional and rural news agencies and gift stores who have approached us and with whom we negotiated a competitive commission rate. The Rural Book Shop, with Fairfax Media, also approached us and has taken a sizeable consignment.

We have taken stalls at events for rural women, including Weengallon Ladies Day, Women in Ag Day at Jimbour, and the

2018 Queensland Rural Regional and Remote Women's Network Conference. We received invitations to be guest speakers at Tattersall's Ladies High Tea in Brisbane, and the Kimberley Pilbara Cattlemen's Association Ladies Lunch. My trip to Broome was most unexpected and most exciting!

Media opportunities have also included ABC Radio interviews (Brisbane and Regional Qld) as well as in Fairfax's *Queensland Country Life* newspaper and New Corp Australian's *Rural Weekly*. Extracts have been published in other agricultural magazines and publications. Again, all approaches have come to us.

Our best advice to new authors: Know your target audience and focus your energy there. Go to events where they are, and promote your story and the book's message in ways that reach those people through newspapers, magazines, television, podcast interviews, website articles, social media and word of mouth.

Footnote: In November 2018 Buckingham Palace wrote to the writer of the Foreword, Jane Thomas, thanking her for gifting the book to HRH The Princess Royal (Princess Anne) at the Royal Agricultural Show Society's Biennial Conference in Edmonton, Canada. You never know to whom or where your book will go.

www.cattlemeninpearls.com

*If something inside of you is real, we will probably find it interesting, and it will probably be universal. So you must risk placing real emotion at the center of your work. Write straight into the emotional center of things. Write toward vulnerability. Risk being unliked. Tell the truth as you understand it.*

~ Anne Lamott in *Bird by Bird: Some Instructions on Writing and Life*

## CHAPTER 14

# MEDIA AND SPEAKING

The success of your book is up to you. As well as getting it into the hands of readers through personal contact, sales, events, gifting, and more, it's the ideal time to step into the spotlight yourself, through speaking gigs, media interviews, podcast guest spots, and more.

Thousands of books are published every week, so your new book is probably not a news story on its own – unless you are noteworthy in other areas. So, where is your story?

Earlier in this book I asked you to dig deep and identify how you and your book add value to a bigger discussion in the world before you even begin to write. That is now where the story lies.

Regional, state and national media companies may be keen to feature you and your book if you connect with a larger issue of interest to a sizeable part of their audience. For example, if you've written a book on small business, you may be a credible authority during a story on government funding options for business, providing insightful comments on this national issue from a local perspective.

This book, for example, is not newsworthy. The purpose of the book, however, is to encourage women to step into the spotlight and take ownership of their expertise. To become vocal and visible – and proud. To be successful and financially independent. To be present in decision-making circles.

We live in a society in Australia where women are still struggling for equal pay; where intelligent women are bullied in our Parliament until they choose to leave their hard-earned political posts; where women are starting businesses in increasing numbers because they feel invisible in the corporate space; where smart women are bullied or abused at home. Do you think my deeper message has a place in a larger story?

Definitely. As the author of this book I could speak about those higher level issues within my space in an authoritative way.

Does that lead directly to book sales? No, but it leads to impact, influence, presence, profile, and more open doors to do good work – which is the true purpose of our books anyway.

# HOW TO GAIN MEDIA ATTENTION

Use press releases to generate interest in the bigger story, and offer to be a source of commentary or a case study. Better still, send a done-for-you story in your release.

When I launched *Work from Home* magazine, an evening television current affairs show at that time, *Today Tonight*, picked up my media release within a day. They ran a story that week about the growing home-based business trend at that time, and filmed the three examples of home-based business owners I gave to them – one of which was me. I had provided them with an instant story.

Similarly, based on another of my press releases a few years later, *Brisbane Extra* (no longer running) quickly featured my magazine for mature women starting a business, *Honestly Woman*. In the story that aired, they linked together *Menopause the Musical*, which was playing in Brisbane at the time; the concept of post-menopausal zest (PMZ) as defined by Margaret Mead; and three case studies of women over 50 starting new businesses – a growing trend – who I presented in my media release. I was one of the three and became a part of an interesting topical story.

That format worked well – a topical issue, a voice of authority, and three accessible case studies.

The real benefits of that exposure were profile and credibility. Sales of the magazines did not spike overnight, but viewers became aware of the publications and of my deeper messages about enterprise and independence. The ongoing impact showed up as speaking engagements, content offers for the magazine, partnerships, business credibility, recognition on a national level – and several business awards.

## ANOTHER MEDIA RELEASE THAT WORKED

While publishing *Honestly Woman* magazine I turned a friend's small media release about her new native flower growing business into a bigger story about the $40 million-a-year import of flowers into Australia, when local growers like Lana struggled to be seen. That story was very well received by the media and was her springboard to a much more prominent profile, then a lot of industry and training involvement at a high level, and later a state-level agricultural award.

It's important to think strategically about how you can add a voice to, or a perspective on, the bigger issues that the media wants to cover for their specific audience.

Start paying attention when authors present on television or appear in the weekend newspapers or magazines, and look more deeply to see why the media chose to interview that particular author. What is it about the author, their book, and their key messages that are interesting? How has the media story connected their book to a bigger issue?

# HOW DO YOU FIND THE RIGHT MEDIA PEOPLE TO CONTACT?

Subscribe to media services such as SourceBottle (www. sourcebottle.com), Media Connections (www.mediaconnectioins. com.au), and MediaConnect (www.mediaconnect.com.au) because media people use such platforms to call for expertise and commentary relevant to stories they work on from time to time.

Many journalists use Twitter to watch for potential stories and call out for sources.

Use LinkedIn to find publications and staff, and make contact.

Use online media release distribution services such as Handle Your Own PR; PRWire, Medianet, Get the Word Out, and more.

Search online for podcasts with an audience of people in your target readership and reach out.

# AUTHOR PR

You might choose to invest in an author publicity (PR) service to work with you for a period of time after your book is released, to raise your profile in the media. Be aware that this may not lead to a quick spike in sales, so be prepared to work hard and spread the word about any media coverage you receive, with the intention of raising your profile, authority and credibility. Good things can flow from that.

Take a look at Helen Baker's website to see how that is done well. Helen is a Brisbane-based financial adviser (see page 224) who has focussed her desire to support women to be financially independent in her two books, *On Your Own Two Feet* and *On Your Own Two Feet - Divorce*. Her website is found at www.onyourowntwofeet.com.au.

# AUTHOR MEDIA KIT

The purpose of a media kit is to provide information to media outlets, news desk managers, journalists, publicists, and other potential interviewers, with a goal to secure a useful conversation. It should include:

- ☐ Contact details
- ☐ Bio
- ☐ Media release
- ☐ Sample Q&A/ Tips sheet: this helps interviewers by providing 7-10 questions and sample answers you prepared earlier
- ☐ Photos of you and your book cover, separately. Provide both 72dpi and 300dpi versions.
- ☐ Recent news coverage
- ☐ Book details including title, author, genre, audience, ISBN, publication date, synopsis, availability, testimonials/reviews
- ☐ Sample of your book – downloadable

# SPEAKING OPPORTUNITIES

As an author you may receive many and varied opportunities to speak when you prepare well and let the world know you are available. The level of events will vary according to your current speaking skill, profile, topic, and availability, from local business networking meetings to international conferences.

If speaking is a skill you wish to develop, I suggest you search local or online speaking resources, training coaches and programs, and groups such as Toastmasters.

Start at a level you are comfortable with, seek out speaking opportunities, and don't be afraid to stretch yourself – say yes, and figure out how, if offered something in the fear zone. You will have the material – it's just a matter of reducing it to a shorter, targeted conversation.

And as always, while you are waiting for invitations, make it happen yourself. Plan your own online and in-person events, or co-plan with others with a similar audience, and speak at those.

# AUTHOR SPEAKER KIT

The purpose of this is to provide information to meeting planners, event organisers, speaker bureaus and agencies, or podcasters, with a goal to secure speaking opportunities of benefit to others. It should include:

- ☐ Contact details
- ☐ Bio
- ☐ Speaking topics and descriptions
- ☐ Speaking testimonials
- ☐ Photos of you and your book cover, separately. Provide both 72dpi and 300dpi versions.
- ☐ Recent speaking engagements
- ☐ Recent news coverage and/or awards
- ☐ Book details including title, author, genre, audience

---

*In the next exercise make some notes about the higher level issues your work and your book help address.*

# JOURNAL EXERCISE

## BE SEEN

Don't wait until you are an author to seek media coverage and speaking opportunities.

In the work you do, what larger issue are you helping people deal with?

Think about how you can gain media coverage locally, and further afield, right now.

If you don't have a Speaker Kit, begin writing notes about what it will contain.

# HELEN BAKER

*Author of* On Your Own Two Feet *and* On Your Own Two Feet – Divorce, *Helen is a financial adviser and business owner, and founder of the charity 'sixty-one'. She is based in Brisbane, Queensland.*

My main motivation for writing a book was to help women in the first world gain independence with my financial planning knowledge, and to use the proceeds to help women in the third world who are disadvantaged.

My biggest obstacle with my first book, *On Your Own Two Feet – Steady Steps to Women's Financial Independence*, was not knowing where and how to start. I knew I had important content and a ready audience, and I realised I needed help. I engaged Bev Ryan as my book coach, and she helped me understand the overall process and the first step: planning the structure. As I then wrote the content, the book came to life.

I also struggled at first to find the time to write, as I run a busy financial planning practice, so I decided to come into the office one or two hours early each day and just pound away at the keyboard. That time was totally dedicated to getting the first draft done and I found I could generally type a chapter each session. I didn't feel it had to be perfect. I knew the editor would help me take care of that later.

I kept my book project to myself, taking the heat off so I could go at my own pace until it was done. I also decided to avoid looking at anything anyone else had written so I could do it my way, rather than feel influenced or overwhelmed.

With a project management background, I understood that there were many steps involved in publishing, and I reached out for the expertise I needed. Although it's good to do things yourself, it's also wise to know when to delegate unfamiliar tasks and do what you do best instead.

I decided to use high-heel shoe imagery to help make finance fun: it was different, and it didn't look or read like a normal finance book, which was my wish.

Initially I think others saw my first book as a greater achievement than I did, though after hearing so many people say, 'wow, you did it when so many people only talk about it' I began to see it as something special.

I have been blessed with many opportunities since publishing. I have been included in an Australian Women's Weekly feature publication about wealth; I speak at women's events in Australia and overseas; I speak on radio shows regularly; I write columns; and provide expert commentary to the media.

I know the book has inspired and motivated women to make pivotal changes, and that's really valuable and exciting to me. You never know who your book touches, where it goes, and what lives might change because of it.

In 2018 I released my second book *On Your Own Two Feet – Divorce* and was invited to speak at the European Family Law Conference held in Paris in September that year.

I see my books as symbols for others who also have big dreams. You can do the same thing with anything in your own life.

www.onyourowntwofeet.com.au

*Your art is what you do when no one can tell you exactly how to do it. Your art is the act of taking personal responsibility, challenging the status quo, and changing people. I call the process of doing your art 'the work'.*

~ Seth Godin,
in *Linchpin: Are You Indispensable?*

## CHAPTER 15

# EXPAND AND ELEVATE

Your book is a low-cost gateway for readers to get a glimpse of you and your expanded business model. As you bring your book into being, you will begin to see the potential laid out before you.

As a business owner or self-employed professional who has been learning and improving as you trade your expertise for money, you are probably sitting on a mountain of value.

Use your book content as foundation for a more detailed publishing and marketing system that will bring even more value and information to people who now know, like and trust you (because they read your book).

Some will want access to a deeper level of learning and support from you, because not everyone can make big changes on their own. Don't assume that because you explained 'how to' in your book, all readers will simply go do. Some will want more in-depth information, encouragement, accountability, a schedule, an ongoing cheer squad, answers to questions as they arise, and access to other ideas and skills. You can provide this in various e-learning formats, live interaction, and/or a combination of both, and reach a far greater number of people than you do now.

Some will also pay you to implement changes on their behalf – a much higher value service.

## PLAY BETTER

You will have seen many business owners very successfully apply this strategy and create multiple streams of ongoing income, change the way they work, and simply play on a much bigger scale.

Others refine their lives after a high-pressured career, and create a new lifestyle and business they feel is more meaningful and rewarding.

Get clear on your own dreams and accept that all of the supposedly successful names in the field of product and program publishing and marketing began somewhere. They started where they were, worked hard (and still do), made mistakes, lost money, picked themselves up, learned from others doing it right, invested in themselves, eventually understood their customers' reasons for buy-in, made money, and persisted.

I suggest that you find people doing what you would like to do, and apply some of their principles in your own world, at a level you enjoy.

You could even interview them to gather their stories for your book, LinkedIn article, blog, podcast or newsletter.

**Here are a few examples:**

*www.janeteresa.com with Jane Teresa Anderson, BSc Hons and dream analyst:* Her interest in dreams grew from her study of neurophysiology, and her first book, *Sleep On It*, was published in 1994. Today she is a frequent media guest, podcaster, author of seven books, mentor, international consultant, educator, and creator of The Dream Academy.

*www.changinghabits.com.au with Cyndi O'Meara, nutritionist, now filmmaker, author, international speaker, and life-changing coach:* Her book, *Changing Habits, Changing Lives*, was first published in 1998 and her profile and business grew from that point. Today her online business sells food, health and wellbeing products; books; health programs; audios and DVDs … and more.

*www.happylawyerhappylife.com with family lawyer, Clarissa Rayward:* Her first book *Splitsville* raised her profile and began the transformation of Clarissa's family law practice, while her second book, *Happy Lawyer Happy Life*, opened up another very successful business stream – her mastermind, life and business programs for entrepreneurial lawyers.

# UPLEVEL

Here are the most popular methods of producing, purposing, and packaging your knowledge for ongoing sales:

### On-demand courses

You can develop and record short courses that cover each step in your process separately and sell them individually; or longer courses that cover more content in a single download, or a series of downloads. The accepted price range may be $50 to $2000 depending on content and perceived value.

### Programs

This model is a combination of structured learning material and a personal mentor or guide, and has the highest profit margin, often priced from $3000 upward. Provide high-value content, a definite process, and expert support to move people from knowledge through to implementation then transformational results, and your programs may be well priced in the 5-figure zone – and upward from there as you build a bank of success.

### Membership model

This involves creating a community where people may pay from $10/month up to $250/month, depending on the perceived value. As attractive as this model seems, it requires a large amount of content generation and ongoing production. Your profit margin per person over 12 months will be higher than that of a sale of your book, of course, but you will have to work all year to gain that.

## OTHER PRODUCTS AND SERVICES TO CONSIDER

### Speaking

Keynotes, workshops, facilitation, event MC/host, training, telecoaching.

### Products

Webinar and training recordings, videos, printed products, merchandise, co-marketing of other people's products compatible with your purpose.

### Publications

Print and digital magazines, books, e-books, card sets, workbooks, mini-books, series, customised content for various audiences, other people's products.

**Events**

Networking events, recurring group meetings, masterminds, retreats, workshops, webinars, trade shows, VIP events, client events, conferences.

**Consulting**

Charge a fee for services assisting others within your areas of expertise.

**Technology**

Work with skilled people to develop apps, web portals, and other online services for your audience.

———————

*In the next exercise, spend some time making notes about how you might use your book for leverage.*

# JOURNAL EXERCISE

## LEVERAGE

What ideas do you have for ongoing events, products and services that will help the people you like to work with get what *they* really want?

Of all of the options available to you, which would you really love to do?

How can you begin soon?

*Once you make the decision you will find all the people, resources, and ideas you need every time.*

~ Bob Proctor

# CONCLUSION

Dear Reader,

I trust you are now confident that you too can publish a quality book that will expand you and your business – even though you may not see yourself as a writer, and you have questioned how a book could fit with your business in the past.

Keep these steps in mind, and they will guide you well:

> *Make a decision! That simple act alone unlocks doors and invites all you need to come to you.*

> *Know your clients – people with a strong desire for results, who are willing and able to invest in attaining those results.*

> *Focus your business on serving these people and provide value to them.*

> *Work with a book coach to properly plan and write the book that positions you as a leader in your field.*

*Gather a cheer squad around you, to keep you accountable and positive.*

*Access a quality book production team when the time comes.*

*Use your book cover, book title and sub-title, testimonials and back section to attract the right people, and meaningful connections.*

*Then provide more value from the heart, always be helpful, champion your people, learn what they truly want, and empower them to achieve.*

I invite you now to connect with me personally so I can provide more value and assistance to you over time. You will find my contact points below and on the next page.

To your book success!

Bev Ryan

E: bev@bevryanpublish.com
W: www.smartwomenpublish.com
LI: www.linkedin.com/in/bevryan
IG: smart_women_publish
FB: www.facebook.com/BevRyanPublishing

# PUBLISHING ASSISTANCE

**YOUR FREE EXTRAS:** Go to www.smartwomenpublish.com/extras to download a Publishing Process Diagram; a Book Deadline Wall Chart; a Book Business Plan; and a Book Cover Checklist mentioned in this book.

**BOOK COACHING:** Do you need help planning and kick-starting your book? Go to www.smartwomenpublish.com/book-coaching

**PUBLISHING SERVICES:** Have you almost completed your manuscript, and require an editor, cover and page designer, printer and e-book creator? Go to www.smartwomenpublish.com/publish

**SPEAKER & WORKSHOP PRESENTER:** Do you require a speaker or presenter at networking events, women's events or training/professional development days? Contact Bev Ryan at bev@bevryanpublish.com.

**SMART WOMEN PUBLISHING EVENTS & NEWS**
Go to www.smartwomenpublish.com to opt in and receive coming author profiles, events, programs, and publishing information.

# REFERENCES

*The range of publishing dates in the list below
attests to the impact and longevity of books.*

**Foreword**

Frankel, Lois P Phd. International coach, speaker and author: drloisfrankel.com

**Introduction**

Gilbert, Elizabeth. Author: elizabethgilbert.com
Sher, Barbara. *I could do anything if only I knew what it was*, Bantam Dell, 1999

**Chapter 1**

Gregory, Patt. *Woodwork for Women*: woodworkforwomen.com.au
*The NBN™ Silver Economy Report*, NBN Co Ltd, 2017
La Porte, Danielle. Author: daniellelaporte.com
Leighton, Maryanne. *Equine Emergency Rescue – a guide to Large Animal Rescue*, 2012

**Chapter 2**

Galloway, Anne (Publisher). *Cattlemen in Pearls – Celebrating Women in Agriculture*, 2018

Nielsen BookScan. Publishing data provider: npd.com/industry-expertise/books

The Book Depository. UK-based online book seller: bookdepository.com

Booktopia. Australian-based online book seller: booktopia.com.au

Association of American Publishers. Trade association of the American book publishing industry: publishers.org

Australian Federation of Graduate Women Inc: australiangradwomen.org.au

Kerr, Lisa-Marie. *Get Job Ready: A teen's guide to getting their first job,* 2012

Hanckel, Jane. *Growing Greener Children:* inspirededucation.com.au

## Chapter 3

Klauser, Henriette Anne. *Write It Down, Make It Happen.* Touchstone Books, 2001

Spera, Buhrfeind and Pennebaker. 'Expressive Writing and Coping with Job Loss', 1994: jstor.org/stable/256708

Brook, Karen. Coach and Proctor Gallagher Consultant: karenbrook.com.au

Boulton, Maria MD. *Mum's Guide to Pregnancy*: drmariaboulton.com.au

## Chapter 4

Jansen, Julie. *I Don't Know What I Want, But I Know It's Not This: A Step-by-Step Guide to Finding Gratifying Work.* Penguin Books. Revised 2016

Buckingham, Marcus. *Discover Your Strengths.* Gallup Press, 2005

Brien, DL and Brady, T. *Girl's Guide to Real Estate.* Allen & Unwin, 2002

Priestly, Daniel. *Become a Key Person of Influence.* Rethink Press, 2014

Winter, Barbara. *Making a Living Without a Job.* Bantam Dell, 2009

Tate, Carolyn. *The Purpose Project.* Carolyn Tate & Co, 2017

Google Analytics. Web analytics service: analytics.google.com/analytics/web

*O Magazine.* American monthly magazine: oprah.com/app/o-magazine.html

Nash, Jennie. CEO of Author Accelerator: jennienash.com

## Chapter 5

Hodges, Kathryn. *Who Gets the Dog?* 2016

## Chapter 6

Bhargava, Rohit. *Personality Not Included: Why Companies Lose Their Authenticity–And How Great Brands get It Back.* McGraw Hill, 2008

Godin, Seth. Author: sethgodin.com

Franklin, Christine. *The Extra Mile: The Essential Guide for Health Professionals Going Bush.* 2017

## Chapter 7

Kleon, Austin. *Steal Like An Artist.* Workman, 2012

Ryan, Bev. *Smart Women Publish.* 2019

Heath, C and Heath D. *Made to Stick: Why Some Ideas Survive and Others Die.* 2007

Carnegie, Dale. *How to Win Friends & Influence People.* Harper Collins, 2016

Holmes, Catherine V. *How to Draw Cool Stuff.* Library Tales Publishing, 2014

Ferris, Tim. *The 4-Hour Work Week.* Vermilion, 2011

Dubner SJ and Levitt SD. *Freakonomics–A Rogue Economist Explores the Hidden Side of Everything.* Harper Collins, 2020

Cain, Susan. *Quiet: The power of introverts in a world that can't stop talking.* Penguin, 2013

Kondo, Marie. *The Life-Changing Magic of Tidying Up.* Vermilion, 2014

Griffiths, Andrew. *101 Ways to Market Your Business.* Allen & Unwin, 2006

Cover, Stephen R. *The 7 Habits of Highly Effective People (30th Anniversary Edition).* Simon & Schuster, 2020

Ware, Bronnie. *The Top Five Regrets of the Dying.* Hay House, 2019

Chapman, Gary. *The 5 Love Languages.* Strand Publishing, 2015

Wilbur, Todd. *Top Secret Restaurant Recipes–the series.*

Froelich, Paula. *It! Nine Secrets of the Rich and Famous That Will Take You to the Top.* Miramax Books, 2006

Gilbert, Elizabeth. *Eat, Pray, Love*. Riverhead Books, 2010

Obama, Michelle. *Becoming*. Viking, 2018

Wamariya, Clementine. *The Girl Who Smiled Beads*. Windmill Books, 2019

McBride, Sarah. *Tomorrow Will be Different*. Crown, 2019

Canfield, Jack. *Chicken Soup* series of books, HCI

Galloway, Anne (Publisher). *Cattlemen in Pearls – Celebrating Women in Agriculture*, 2018

Abercrombie, Barbara. *Cherished–21 Writers on Animals They Have Loved and Lost*. New World Library, 2011

Reagan Noon, Colleen. *InFertility–Secrets, Struggles and Successes*. Bowker, 2021

Salzberg, Sharon. *Real Happiness*. Workman Publishing, 2011

Lamott, Anne. *Bird by Bird*. Anchor, 1995

Thorpe-Bowker Australia ISBN and barcodes: myidentifiers.com.au

National Library of Australia cataloguing: nla.gov.au

Bartolini, Tanya. *Blending the Cultures*. 2013

## Chapter 8

Talent Dynamics profiling model: tdprofiletest.com

Hamilton, Roger. Wealth Dynamics: wealthdynamics.com

Sher, Barbara. *Wishcraft–How To Get What You Really Want*. Ballantine Books, 2004

Sher, Barbara. Success Teams: shersuccessteams.com

Grieve, Jane. *Slippin' on the Lino* and *In Stockmen's Footsteps*: janegrieve.com.au

## Chapter 9

Beck, Martha. Sociologist, life coach, best-selling author: marthabeck.com

Londolozi. South African game reserve: londolozi.com

Simmons, Viti Kay. *A Tree Needs Water to Bear Fruit*. Bearing Fruit–Microfinance. *Hikoi of Discovery*: bearfruit.com.au

Larson, Erik. *The Devil in the White City.* Bantam UK, 2004

Gilbert, Elizabeth. *Big Magic–Creative Living beyond Fear.* Bloomsbury, 2016

Roche, Amy. *The Retail Experiment.* Michael Hanrahan Publishing, 2017

## Chapter 10

Simmons, Annette. *The Story Factor.* Basic Books, 2019

Cron, Lisa. *Wired for Story.* Clarkson Potter, 2012

Cron, Lisa. *Story Genius: How to Use Brain Science to Go Beyond Outlining and Write a Riveting Novel.* Clarkson Potter, 2016

Cron, Lisa. *Story or Die: How to Use Brain Science to Engage, Persuade, and Change Minds in Business and in Life.* Ten Speed Press, 2021

Hamilton, Felicity. *Accreditation Ready: Smart Strategies for Successful Stress-Free Audits.* OneVault, 2018

Orr, Geoff. *Your Future–Shape It: 6 Steps to Financial Peace of Mind.* Java, 2016

Gibbons, Denise. *Women as Leaders: The World Needs You.* Denise Gibbons, 2017

Barret, Kris. *High Thrive Me! A 5-step guide to helping kids with autism live happier, healthier lives*: Kris Barret, 2016

Cummins, Dolores. *Altitude–Two Women's Journey on Mt Kilimanjaro*: dolorescummins.com

## Chapter 11

Knapp, Kate. Australian author and artist, and creator of Twigseeds: twigseeds.com

Publishizer. Book crowdfunding platform and literary agency: publishizer.com

Jennings, Beth. *Memories at Your Fingertips* and *She knows*: bethjenningsphotography.com

## Chapter 12

ISBN & barcodes: myidentifiers.com.au

Publish on Amazon Kindle: kdp.amazon.com/en_US

Apple Books for authors: authors.apple.com

IngramSpark for authors: ingramspark.com

Woodslane book distribution in Australia: woodslane.com.au

John Reed Books: johnreedbooks.com.au

Australian Society of Authors: asauthors.org

Booktopia Publishing Services: publisherservices.com.au

Reid, Bronwyn. *Small Company, Big Business* and *Small Company, Big Crisis*: bronwynreid.com.au

## Chapter 13

Simmons, Viti Kay. Author and social entrepreneur: bearfruit.com.au

Franklin, Christine. Psychologist and author of *The Extra Mile*: sybellahealth.com.au

Godin, Seth. Author: sethgodin.com

Goins, Jeff. Writer: goinswriter.com

Rush, Callan. *Wealth Through Workshops:* callanrush.com

Grahl, Tim. Author and author coach. *Your First 1000 Copies*: booklaunch.com

Galloway, Anne (Publisher). *Cattlemen in Pearls – Celebrating Women in Agriculture*: cattlemeninpearls.com

## Chapter 14

SourceBottle: sourcebottle.com

Media Connections: mediaconnectioins.com.au

MediaConnect: mediaconnect.com.au

Handle Your Own PR: handleyourownpr.com.au

PRWire: prwire.com.au

Medianet: medianet.com.au

Get the Word Out: getthewordout.com.au

Baker, Helen. *On Your Own Two Feet – Divorce*: onyourowntwofeet.com.au

## Chapter 15

Anderson, Jane Teresa. Dream analyst and author: janeteresa.com

O'Meara, Cyndi. Nutritionist and author: changinghabits.com.au

Rayward, Clarissa. Lawyer, author and coach: happylawyerhappylife.com